THE WORLD OF
A TREE

THE WORLD OF A
TREE

Arnold Darlington

M.A., M.B.O.U., F.I. Biol.
Head of the Biology Department
Malvern College

Photographs by
Arnold Darlington

Drawings by
Wilhelmina Mary Guymer

FABER AND FABER
3 Queen Square
London

First published in 1972
by Faber and Faber Limited
3 Queen Square London WC1
Photoset by
BAS Printers Limited
Wallop, Hampshire
Printed in Great Britain by
Latimer Trend & Co Ltd Whitstable

ISBN 0 571 09624 7

To the memory of the Quaker botanist and farmer

JOSHUA LAMB
(1856–1943)

of Sibford Ferris, Oxfordshire, who never felled an oak-tree without planting acorns to replace it and whose oaks are now themselves bearing fruit.

Your ghost will walk, you lover of trees,
(If our loves remain)
In an English lane.

ROBERT BROWNING

The writer acknowledges with gratitude the co-operation of Mr. C. H. Torrance, Headmaster of Hillstone School, Malvern, for permitting five of his boys—Christopher Bradley-Kidd, Christopher Pedlar, Nicholas Rowe, Andrew Severn and John Swallow—to undertake the practical work illustrated here.

Contents

Illustrations

PLATES

FIGURES

1. Read this first

What our book is about

It tells a true story—one of the most wonderful stories there is to tell. It is the story of one kind of tree and how the lives of numerous animals and plants are involved with it. Although the particular tree is the oak, we might have spun our story around other kinds instead. All trees are important. All of them become a sort of focus for living things—here we call it a 'world'. Unfortunately, many people either do not realise this, or forget it, and cut down trees which could be preserved.

Some are people who have a passion for tidiness. They would rather see a tarred sidewalk with kerbs than a verge of wild flowers, or a chain hanging from a row of posts than a hedgerow. No doubt such objects look trim, but they are really man-made deserts. On the other hand, where there are oak-trees, great numbers of living things find shelter, food, and somewhere to breed. In fact, the world of an oak is probably bigger than the world of any other kind of tree.

Perhaps parts of the story seem cruel to us. For instance, the way in which some of the attackers mentioned on page 108 dwell inside their victims and slowly eat them alive. We need to remember that an animal does not have the protection we get

13

from our intelligence and elaborate social system. It considers no living thing of any other kind. Most of its time has to be spent searching for food merely to stay alive. Like many a human being—who should know better—it is a 'mick on the make'.

Those names

We may find the names used in our book difficult at first. Some of them are certainly difficult to pronounce (and spell). People often call them Latin names. This is not quite accurate. Some of the words come from other languages—Greek for example. They are scientific names. In a few cases, we are translating them to show what they mean. We need to ask ourselves why scientists use them. There are several reasons. Here are three of them.

Firstly, the names are international, and scientists all over the world can understand them.

Secondly, its scientific name tells us more about a living thing than does its English name. The first part of its name shows the group to which it belongs and indicates its close relatives.

Thirdly, English names can be so misleading that we dare not rely on them even in Britain. For example, on page 137 we mention the bluebell. But a bluebell to an Englishman is not a bluebell to a Scotsman. When a Scotsman speaks of bluebells he means different plants altogether. The 'bluebells of Scotland' are what the English call harebells. They are not even related and do not live in the same kinds of places. The bluebell of England—*Endymion nonscriptus*—occurs in oak-woods. The bluebell of Scotland—*Campanula rotundifolia*—is found in dry and open grassy places.

Where we can, we give both the English and the scientific name. But many animals and plants living among oaks are unfamiliar to the general public and have received no English names that have caught on.

The sizes of things

It is difficult to judge the real sizes of organisms from pictures if we are not familiar with them. We are trying to overcome the problem by including figures of oak-leaves where we can. All leaves vary, but a large oak-leaf is about 100 mm long. This is the length of those in our illustrations. They will help us to gain a rough idea of the sizes of other living things nearby.

Further reading

A book of our kind cannot go into detail about all the forms of life it mentions. After reading it, we may become interested in certain groups and wish to find out more about them. We need to consult other books for this. The list on page 145 will help us.

2. The start of it all

The common oak

More than a hundred different kinds (species) of trees and bushes grow wild in Britain. Oak-trees are some of the commonest. And we have four principal species of oaks. Two of them the Romans must have seen when they settled here. These are native species. But two they could not have found growing here because we know that these species were introduced from abroad centuries after the Romans had gone.

The sweet chestnut, whose fruits we eat (but *not* the horse chestnut, whose conkers are quite unfit to eat), the beech and the oaks, belong to one family of plants. All of them produce nuts (hard fruits) in little cups. Oaks form a particular group— a genus—inside this family. Because the genus is named *Quercus*, oaks have scientific names beginning with this one. It is a sort of surname, although it is put first. Thus, our four oaks are called, the pedunculate oak (*Quercus robur*), sessile oak = durmast oak (*Q. petraea*), Turkey oak (*Q. cerris*) and holm oak = evergreen oak (*Q. ilex*). The first two are the native ones. The Turkey and holm oaks are those which were brought from other countries and deliberately planted here. They are still chiefly found in parks and gardens. Here and there, however, we can find them growing wild.

Only the holm oak keeps its foliage all the year round. The others have lost nearly all their leaves by the end of November.

Which of the four kinds of *Quercus* is the 'common' oak? It is unlikely to be one or other of the introduced sort. Perhaps we can narrow it down to one of the native species.

But the question is easier to ask than answer. Although many oaks grow in hedgerows or as lone trees in fields, they also form woods. Such woodlands often develop in different regions and on different soils. Pedunculate oak forms woods on clayey soil which is slightly alkaline. It is the common oak of east and south England and the Midlands. Sessile oak (durmast oak) is commonest in west and north Britain. Its woods grow on lighter, more acid soils. But in some districts the two species are mixed up together. Places where the soil is rather damp and sandy, for instance. And where the two are close together, they sometimes breed together. When this happens they produce *hybrids*.

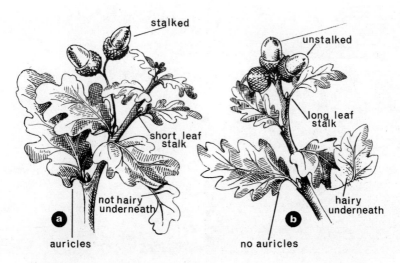

Figure 1. Shoots of the two principal oaks: a. pedunculate oak = common oak (*Quercus robur*), b. sessile oak = durmast oak (*Q. petraea*).

17

The hybrids have features of both parents. They can be hard to identify.

Over the whole of Britain, there are certainly more pedunculate oaks than sessile oaks. Therefore, pedunculate oak is the species which is often called *common* oak. But which is truly the common oak near our home is likely to depend on where we live. As far as this book is concerned, it does not matter very much. Most of the animals and plants live around either of our two native kinds of oak and their hybrids. All the same, it is interesting to try to identify the trees we see.

While we are reading this section, we should turn to the pictures in figure 1 and plates 1 and 2. They will help us with our identifications. *Quercus robur* has its fruits (acorns) in little cups which grow on a long, slender stalk—a *peduncle*. This is why it is called 'pedunculate oak'. But in the sessile oak, the stalk is

Plate 1. Common oak (pedun-culate oak) with domed crown. Height, 40 metres.

Plate 2. Common oak with square crown. Height, 40 metres.

much shorter. In fact, the cup seems to be fastened directly to the twig. And 'sessile' means 'without a stalk'. Then if there are no acorns to be seen, the actual leaves can be examined. Both species have leaves which look much the same, with about 10 rounded lobes along the edges. But pedunculate oak has the flat part of the leaf folded into two tiny 'ears' (auricles) near the leaf-stalk. Leaves of sessile oak have no auricles and are hairy on the underside near the midrib (central vein). And sessile oak has a longer leaf-stalk (1–2 cm) than pedunculate oak (0·5 cm).

Lastly, there is a way of telling them apart from a distance. But we need to be specially careful here. Oaks in woods are usually crowded. They may be cut (coppiced) periodically. Lack of light and some forms of cutting may cause them to grow like leafy poles. Their shapes are of little use for identification. Any trees we choose must have had a chance to grow properly. Oaks standing on their own are likely to be best. Also, they should be large, old trees which have not been cut about very much. Whatever specimens we examine, we notice how the branches of both sorts are bent into 'elbows' and 'knees'. With age, the upper branches of both tend to die back and lose leaves, bark and twigs. The boughs become gaunt and jagged against the sky. They remind us of a stag's antlers and such trees are said to be *stag-headed*. But if we choose very carefully, we find that the pedunculate oak looks heavier than the sessile oak. It has a wider crown (top), either domed or square in outline, and its older branches come off lower down the trunk. Plates 1 and 2 give the shapes of common oaks growing where they are not crowded.

Oaks have a rough bark with deep hollows. Probably most of us have taken the impression of something like a coin, by covering it with paper and rubbing a pencil over it. If we use heelball, which is soft, and copy people who make brass-rubbings

Plate 3. Taking an impression of cherry-bark with heelball.

in churches, we can make a *bark*-rubbing. It allows us to take
the pattern from the bark of a tree without damaging it. Plate
3 shows this being done on a cherry-tree. Rubbings of the bark
of three different species of trees are compared in figures 2–4.
Alternatively, we might make a cast of the bark in plaster-of-
paris. This has the advantage of recording the depth of the
hollows.

Figure 2. Bark-rubbing: oak. Compare with smoother lime and cherry (figs. 3 and 4).

Figure 3. Bark-rubbing: cherry (plate 3).

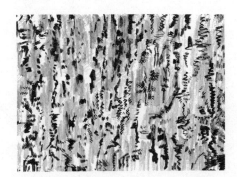

Figure 4. Bark-rubbing: lime

When they are fully grown, oaks can measure up to 16 metres around the trunk at eye-level and be as high as 30–40 metres. Even when a tree is too tall for direct measurement, we are able to estimate its height. There are several ways of doing this. The boys in plate 4 are using a method based on the properties of similar triangles.

Plate 4. Using the properties of similar triangles to estimate a tree's height. Stick is 9 metres, and the nearer boy 10 metres, from the oak. A straight line from his eye to the tree's top intersects the stick. Its vertical height at the stick in decimetres represents the tree's height in metres.

'Tall oaks from little acorns grow'

A man named David Everett wrote this nearly 200 years ago, when he was a schoolboy. He wanted to remind people of something they knew already. But to understand how it happens, we must know how acorns are formed.

Acorns are fruits, not seeds. Perhaps we think of fruits as things which are juicy and tasty. But many fruits are hard like acorns. A single acorn usually has one big seed inside. We can find this by splitting the acorn open with a strong knife. After the acorn has dropped to the ground, the seed inside starts to grow (germinate). Then it splits the acorn naturally.

Fruits and seeds come from flowers. An oak-tree has flowers, but we can easily miss them. They are not brightly coloured like the blossom we see in spring on trees in orchards. Brightly coloured flowers are usually visited by insects, like moths or bees. The insects get food from the flowers and, at the same time, help the flowers to produce fruits and seeds. This is why such flowers are easily seen. They often have a pleasant smell, too. Insects must be able to find them.

But oak-flowers do not use insects in this way. Therefore they have no need of bright colour or scent. They are small, although they grow in clusters. The flowers are of two kinds— male flowers which produce pollen and female flowers which receive it. Instead of insects, they make use of wind.

We find both sorts of flower on the same tree in April and May. Often they are high up. If we cannot reach them, we may manage to pull down a suitable branch with a walking-stick. Figure 5 shows what we should be able to make out, especially if we have a hand-lens.

The male flowers producing the pollen are little bunches of *stamens*. There can be up to eight stamens in each flower. The flowers lie in groups along a thin, dangling stalk. Such an arrangement is a *catkin*. The catkins are easily shaken by gusts

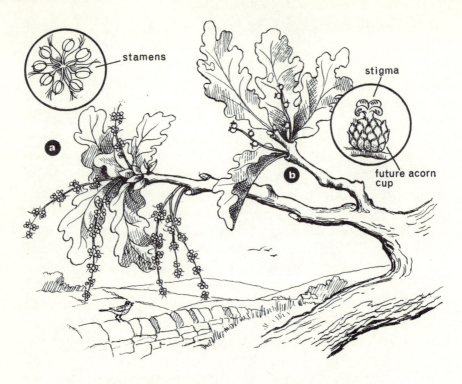

stamens

stigma

future acorn cup

Figure 5. Flowers of oak: a. male, b. female.

of wind. When this happens, pollen-dust coming from the stamens is carried away in the air. After shedding their pollen, the catkins drop off the tree. Great numbers of dead catkins lying on the ground in spring show that reproduction has begun.

The female flowers are not in loose catkins, but in little stiff spikes. There are several flowers in each spike. The most notice-able parts of a single flower are the *stigmas* (something like a star), the *ovary*, and the little *cup* in which the ovary sits. If oak pollen in the wind comes to rest on the stigmas, it causes tiny *ovules* inside the ovaries to turn into seeds. Then the ovary swells until it becomes the acorn (fruit) around the seed (kernel).

24

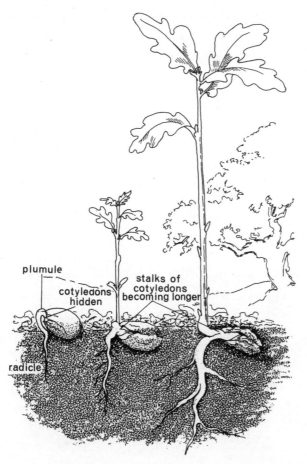

Figure 6. Three stages in the germination and
growth of a young oak (page 26).

Because each ovary contains six ovules, an acorn should contain
six kernels. Nearly always, however, only one of the ovules ever
develops. At the same time, the little cup grows bigger and turns
woody and becomes the acorn cup. Five or six months after
flowering, the acorns are ripe, and they fall from the tree in
September and October.

After they have fallen, their seeds rest for several months. Then they germinate in spring. Every seed contains a store of food which the parent tree has provided. This food is the reason for many animals eating acorns—see chapter 4. The store generally lasts until the young tree (seedling) has grown sufficiently to make food for itself. We can find the food-store by taking a seed apart. There are two fleshy lobes thick with food. These are really special leaves (cotyledons). Between them are two little cones—the young shoot (plumule) and the young root (radicle). When germination takes place, the cotyledons stay underground, but the radicle and plumule emerge from the broken acorn. We may be surprised that the tiny plumule eventually grows into the huge trunk and boughs and the mass of foliage which we see on an old tree.

Oak-trees are fun to grow. All we need are a few acorns and plant-pots. Then we can observe for ourselves the stages shown in figure 6.

And how long shall we have to wait for our seedlings to become old enough to produce their first acorns? This is another of those questions which are easy to ask and hard to answer. We cannot expect them before 10 years, and we might wait until they are 40–50 years old. Probably the situations where they are planted affect the reproduction.

3. *How man uses the oak*

For thousands of years, people in the British Isles have used the oak in many ways. A complete book could be written on the subject. Unfortunately the number of oak-trees in Britain has been going down for centuries. But oaks are still valuable, even though they are not used as much as they were.

'*Heart of oak are our ships*'

David Garrick wrote the song *Heart of Oak* in the eighteenth century, at a time when the British navy was at war. The warships were sailing vessels built of oak. They were the 'wooden walls of the kingdom'. And most of the trees for building them grew here.

Oak was almost ideal. It had three special advantages. It was tough. It could stand exposure to water without going rotten better than most timbers. The strong 'elbows' and 'knees' could be used for shaping the curved part of a ship's stem near the bow.

While the fierce war against Napoleon was being fought, warships were built and repaired in great numbers. More oaks were felled than could be replaced. In a single year, about the time of the Battle of Trafalgar (1805), so much timber was used in the navy that it would have needed an area of land as big as

Plate 5. Common oak, probably over 400 years old, with a trunk 11 metres in circumference.

the county of Rutland to grow it! And more than a thousand oak-trees went into the building of Nelson's *Victory*, a ship 57 metres long, 16 metres wide, and carrying 100 guns.

Eight years before *Victory* was built in 1765, the *Lady Oak* was felled at Minsterley in Shropshire. This huge tree was 15 metres around the trunk. It yielded 66 cu. metres of construction timber and 160 faggots (bundles of fuel). Its wood weighed 17272 kgs. and its stripped-off bark 3448 kgs. It was sold for £10·5. Had it been offered for sale at the time of Trafalgar, its timber alone would have fetched twenty times this amount.

The pound then was worth far more than it is today. Those were the years when fortunes were made by landowners with plenty of oaks to sell. Wars are one reason for there being fewer oaks in modern times. The use of materials has changed so much that vessels are now made of metal or fibreglass. All the same, oak is still used for shipbuilding. Many fishing-boats, for example, are made of it.

Nearly every part of the tree contains *tannic acid* (= tannin). This substance helps to preserve the wood against decay. Where there is exposure to weather, no wood is better. Oak fences, gates, posts, piles, water-wheels and other machinery, and the wooden beams on the outside of old cottages—all last well. Other uses are for wine-barrels; and the supports of bridges and even drinking troughs for animals (plates 6 and 7). The way the timber lasts in water is amazing. Oak-stakes were driven into the bed of the River Thames by Britons to delay the Roman invaders who were trying to cross. Two thousand years later, the stakes were taken out. When they were examined, they were seen to be rotten on the outside but hard and sound on the inside.

Bog-oaks are older still. The wood of these dead trees, preserved in wet peat, is black and very hard. Carvings and ornaments are made from it.

Plate 6. Oak supports standing in a river and carrying a bridge built of conifer wood.

And yet, even the timber of the mighty oak has enemies under water. One of them is the shipworm (*Teredo*). This is really a small shellfish which bores tunnels in wood lying in seawater. Francis Drake's famous ship, *Golden Hind*, was completely destroyed by it.

In ancient buildings, we have oak beams and doors which are nearly a thousand years old. The wood is still made into parquet floors and some kinds of furniture. Our oaks are among the trees whose timber is taken for charcoal-burning. Charcoal is prepared by combusting wood slowly in a limited supply of air. It was particularly important as a fuel in the days before coal-mining. It is still valuable for a variety of purposes. Charcoal prepared from holm oak (=evergreen oak) burns longer than any other kind. And raw oak-timber burns well, too. The yule-

30

Plate 7. Drinking trough made from an oak-trunk.

log, which used to be burned on Christmas Eve, was traditionally an oak-log.

If oak-bark is stripped and crushed, it can be employed for *tanning*. Leather, linen, netting and rope exposed to damp are treated by it. Local industries have been founded on the tannin in oak. Worcester, for example, is a manufacturing centre for gloves. Oaks, which grow plentifully near the city, were originally used for tanning the gloves. Another commercial use for the tannin is mentioned on page 71.

> '*Stretching his brawny arms and leafy hands:*
> *His shade protects the soil, his head the hill commands*'.

The Roman poet who wrote this two thousand years ago was writing about the oak. He was wiser than many people today. Living trees do protect the soil where they are growing. Here are two ways in which this happens. Firstly, the leaves give shade and stop the hot sun drying up the soil. Secondly, their roots bind the soil particles together so that wind or rain do not carry them away. Wind and rain are forces of *erosion*—the gradual wearing-away of soil. Drying makes soil so loose that it is easily eroded.

When trees die and are not replaced, there is a risk of erosion. Wherever we live we generally see examples of erosion: channels cut by rain in slag-heaps, railway-embankments, or heaps of soil in gardens, for instance. These are places where there are few trees protecting the ground.

If we think erosion does not matter, we should remember our crop plants. These grow in rich *topsoil*. And topsoil is the very first layer to be lost by erosion. Here and there—in parts of Scotland, for example—so many trees have been destroyed deliberately that there is serious erosion. Man makes use of oak, and other trees, to prevent erosion, simply by encouraging their growth.

Protection of topsoil is one form of *conservation*. When he undertakes conservation, man makes use of the oak in other ways, too. Nearly always he uses it to provide some kind of cover (shelter). By planting oakwoods, he sets up cover for animals he is trying to breed, including game-birds (pheasants, etc.). By planting hedgerows, he divides his fields and, at the same time, shelters his crops. And where there are oaks in hedges, there is cover for some animals and plants which used to be commoner when oak forests were commoner. Hedgerows sometimes become a last refuge for species of this kind (see page 137).

Many of us know that King Charles the Second hid from his enemies in the branches of an oak-tree after losing the Battle of Worcester. Although this happened only three centuries ago, his oak has disappeared. It could have been destroyed through souvenir-hunters cutting it to pieces.

How man uses the oak

Acorns are not used much by man himself. The seeds have a bitter taste. Nevertheless, acorns have sometimes been eaten by human beings. Mostly this has been at special times, when other food has been scarce. They have been ground up, mixed with meal, and made into a sort of bread. When Napoleon's soldiers were fighting in Spain, they, and the Spaniards, too, ate acorns found in the woods.

More commonly, man has used acorns as fodder for animals. Pigs, for example, used to be fed on them. The right to fatten hogs in oakwoods was called *pannage*. It was a very valuable right a few centuries ago. But changes in farming methods include changes in the way farm animals are fed. Nowadays we have more convenient ways of feeding pigs than by turning them into woods to forage for acorns.

4. *How other animals use the oak*

A. THE SHELTERERS

The oak as a habitat

Living things (organisms) occupy places of many different sorts. The places where they live are their *habitats*. No matter what its habitat may be, any organism needs to get three things from it:
1. Food—including water;
2. Shelter—from weather, enemies, etc.;
3. Somewhere to breed.
If any one of these fails, the organism fails.

Great numbers of organisms depend on the oak. It affects them in various ways, but they are all part of 'the world of a tree'. And figure 7 shows just a few of the inhabitants of such a world. The oak gives them one or more of the three conditions. Some depend on it so completely that they would die out altogether if the oak died out. These include things which need to eat the oak to survive. Others get from it either the second condition (shelter) or the third (somewhere to breed) but not the first (food). If there were no oaks, many of these could probably reach other places and survive there. All that would happen would be that oaks would cease to be part of their habitats.

34

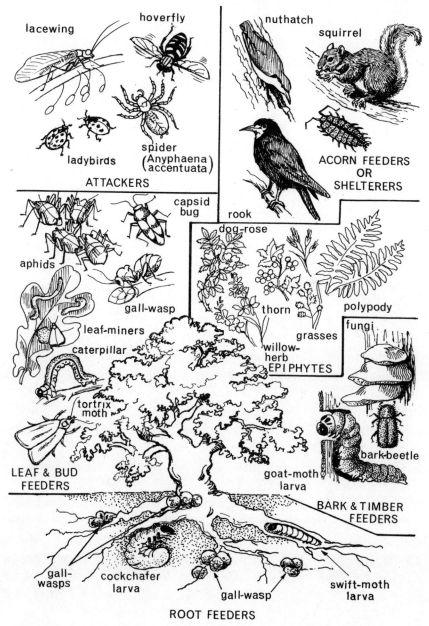

lacewing
hoverfly
ladybirds
spider
(Anyphaena accentuata)
ATTACKERS

nuthatch
squirrel
ACORN FEEDERS
OR
SHELTERERS

capsid bug
rook
dog-rose
aphids
gall-wasp
leaf-miners
caterpillar
thorn
polypody
grasses
willow-herb
EPIPHYTES
fungi
tortrix moth
LEAF & BUD
FEEDERS
goat-moth larva
bark-beetle
BARK & TIMBER
FEEDERS
gall-wasps
cockchafer larva
gall-wasp
swift-moth larva
ROOT FEEDERS

Figure 7. Some of the groups of organisms which depend on oak.

Many organisms, especially animals, use the oak where there is nothing better. But they do not depend on it more closely than this. Some of the most familiar examples are birds. They are also some of the most interesting.

'Well, if you know of a better 'ole, go to it'.

Old Bill was a soldier. He made this remark to a young friend who was always grumbling. Both of them were trying to shelter from gunfire by crouching in a hollow in the ground.

Old Bill's hole suited Old Bill. Decayed hollows in oaks suit many birds. They may shelter here. Some nest here as well. Three species of owls are among them: little owl (*Athene noctua*), tawny owl (*Strix aluco*) and barn owl (*Tyto alba*). All three roost and breed in holes of many sorts.

The little owl is more likely to be found in willow-trees than oaks. And it is more likely to use oaks in hedges than woods. Even if it does not actually nest there, a little owl may regularly use the same hollow for tearing to pieces such prey as rats, mice and voles. The hollow becomes its 'larder'. More tawny owls than little owls use hollow oaks. The barn owl is closely associated with human habitats. Its English name suggests this. When it uses hollow oaks, these are likely to be near farm buildings or even in towns. Occasionally, barn owls have been seen glowing in the dark! They look something like the figures on a luminous watch. These are probably birds which have been in tree-holes. Decaying matter rubbed off by the feathers sometimes glows.

Holes where boughs have broken off may be used by smaller birds. These include the starling (*Sturnus vulgaris*), tree sparrow (*Passer montanus*) and various species of tits. The tree-creeper (*Certhia familiaris*) may nest behind loose bark on the trunk. And though the timber is hard, woodpeckers sometimes drill nesting holes, especially if the tree is diseased. Figure 8d shows how beautifully the hole is made. Like a letter-box, the entrance

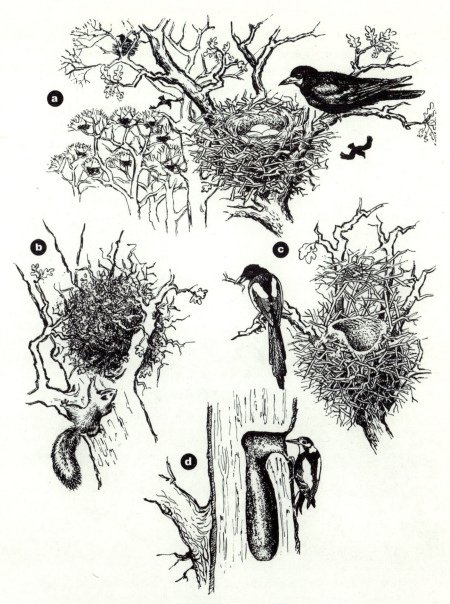

Figure 8. Examples of nests common in oak-trees: a. rook, b. grey squirrel, c. magpie, d. great spotted woodpecker.

is sloped so that rainwater is kept out. No wonder starlings and other birds move in and take over such desirable residences!

When it rains, some holes in oaks do fill with water. These little ponds usually contain rotting wood and leaves. In summer, certain kinds of flies lay their eggs here. The larvae which hatch from the eggs feed on the decaying matter. It is fun to gather some of this and rear the insects in jars at home or school. The maggots may not look particularly attractive. But the flies into which they turn include several with interesting shapes or markings. Figure 9 shows five of them. When they live in tree hollows, they probably benefit from being sheltered. Enemies

Figure 9. Five flies which breed in rotting vegetation: a. *Tipula irrorata* (daddy-long-legs), b. *Dynatosoma fuscicorne* (fungus-gnat), c. *Thereva nobilitata* (stilleto-fly), d. *Helomyza* (helomyzid-fly), e. *Phaonia gobertii* (muscid-fly).

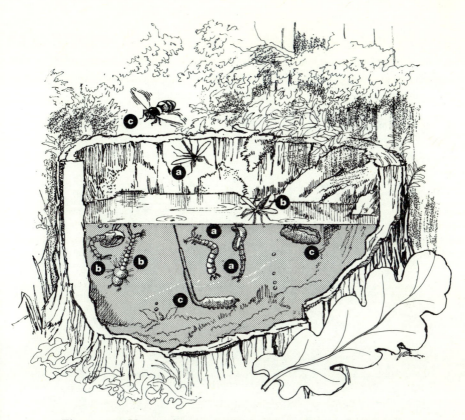

Figure 10. Young insects which can survive in foul water:
a. *Chironomus* (a gnat), b. *Culex* (a gnat), c. *Eristalis* (a hover-fly).
Fresh air is taken in through the water surface.

may miss them, for one thing. But most of these flies are common in more open situations, too.

Not many kinds of flies are restricted to hollows in oaks. Nevertheless we may find some in the oak-tree pools which are. The larvae of gnats and other flies (figure 10) are among those which live in various sorts of water. These include the flooded hollows in oak stumps, and a few gnat species occur hardly anywhere else. Probably decaying wood affects the water and makes it suitable for them. But just because we happen to find

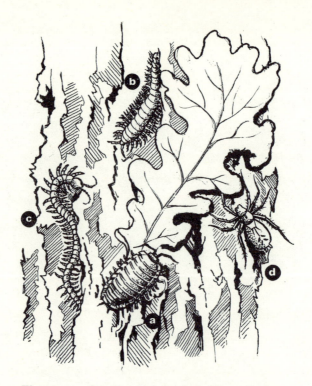

Figure 11. Small animals sheltering within crevices in oak: a. woodlouse, b. millipede, c. centipede, d. spider.

gnat larvae in water-filled stumps, we must not assume that these are kinds which live here and in no other place.

Among the shelterers are animals other than insects. Four of the commonest groups are woodlice, millipedes, centipedes and spiders. They are shown in figure 11. If we search for them, we may notice that the first three seem to be particularly common where it is damp. Rotting wet stumps, for example, or damp places under loose bark. Woodlice, millipedes and centipedes are animals which dry up easily. If this happens, they die. They find shelter where the surrounding air is moist. Although some wander from the protection of their crevices, they generally do so at night, when they are less likely to dry up. But there are exceptions. One common woodlouse species, *Porcellio scaber*, can feed in the open, high up in trees, when the air is warm and dry. It has a protective coating which retains moisture in its body. Woodlice and millipedes are mostly *herbivores* and eat plant matter. They may get food from dead wood. On the other hand, centipedes are *predators* (page 96) which kill other animals. They find their prey in the crevices and elsewhere. Spiders are predators also.

Large animals in the boughs are more noticeable than any of these. Again, birds are what we are most likely to see. Many different species nest in oak branches from time to time. One of them is the rook.

'The many-winter'd crow that leads the clanging rookery home'.

Lord Tennyson was right about one thing when he wrote this. The rook is a kind of crow. Its scientific name, *Corvus frugilegus*, is Latin, and actually means 'the corn-choosing crow'. It may take a few acorns now and then, but it is really a bird of farmlands. Its nests are in colonies (rookeries), nearly always in trees. If we note the trees with rooks' nests in almost any district, we are likely to find oaks among them (see figure 8a).

Look at figure 12, for example. Side-by-side are two pie-charts. They represent the rooks' nests in two counties, Devonshire and Cambridgeshire. Each slice stands for one kind of tree. Its size shows the proportion in it of the nests.

In both counties, rooks mainly use trees of three kinds—oak, elm and ash. Devonshire has many tall trees. Here rooks use the oak a good deal. There are not such big differences between the slices as in Cambridgeshire. The birds have more choice. One feature of Cambridgeshire is that fewer tall trees grow there (see also page 138). Elms are the chief ones. Oak and ash are used

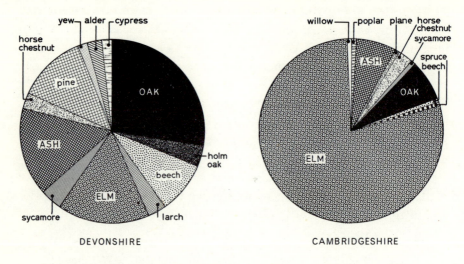

Figure 12. Pie-charts comparing numbers of rooks' nests among occupied trees in two counties.

much less than in Devonshire, and other trees are used very little.

What seems to happen is that rooks generally nest in the tallest trees they can find, whatever these may be. They build their nests as far above the ground as possible. It would be interesting for us to construct similar charts for the rookeries near our own home or school.

Other members of the crow family make use of the oak. The jackdaw (*Corvus monedula*) may nest in its holes—and many jackdaw colonies seem to be established near to rookeries. Like the rook, the magpie (*Pica pica*) usually builds its nest where there are small twigs. It cements the twigs together with mud and works them into the actual structure of the nest (see figure

42

8c). In a sense, it invented reinforced concrete long before human engineers did. On the other hand, the carrion-crow (*Corvus corone*) sets its nest lower down, in a stout fork where there are big boughs.

A wood-pigeon (*Columba palumbus*) uses many situations. It may nest in oak-tree branches or in ivy growing up the trunk. The sparrowhawk (*Accipiter nisus*) often appears inside oak-woods or near to them. It is more likely to nest in a spruce than an oak-tree. Nevertheless, it uses the cover of oaks and other trees to attack small birds (see also page 98).

Not all the nests in oak-branches are those of birds. The grey squirrel (*Sciurus carolinensis*) commonly builds its nests (dreys) in broad-leaved trees (see figure 8b). A drey is shaped like a large,

Plate 8. The ends of a safety-rope secured by a bowline-knot.

Plate 9. Safety-rope in use.

rough ball and is made of leafy twigs. There is a hidden entrance at the side. Although grey squirrels take acorns, much of their food comes from things other than oaks. Often they are destructive predators. The trees they occupy may only be shelters. And smaller mammals—voles, field-mice, etc.—shelter in hollows near the roots.

Generally we have to climb high into a tree if we wish to examine these nests closely. Many of us enjoy climbing trees. But if there are few branches within reach for hand-holds, it is sensible to have a safety-rope or belt. It may slow us up, but we are unlikely to slip. A light nylon rope is one kind which is useful. The thin rope in plates 8 and 9 is so strong it can hold a

44

dead weight of 300 kgs without breaking. It is passed both round the waist and the tree-trunk. Obviously the knot we make to tie the ends together is important. A granny might slip and cause a nasty accident. If tied properly, the *bowline* is safe, and the boy in the photographs is using one. Although the pictures may guide us, we should read a manual on tying knots and practise beforehand if we intend going aloft.

Four of the nest structures mentioned here are shown in figure 8.

B. THE ACORN-FEEDERS

What do we mean?

Before we conclude that a particular animal is an acorn-feeder, we need to think carefully. Do we mean that it generally lives on acorns or simply that it can eat them without being poisoned? Acorns are dangerous to very few of the animals which *could* swallow them. They may be distasteful. The animals may not be able to digest them properly. But they are seldom actually poisonous to them. Some animals take them when there is a shortage of the food which suits them better. Man is one example (see page 33). Others take them more frequently, so that acorns are part of their regular diet. In this book, we are mostly concerned with the 'regulars'.

To deal successfully with an acorn, an animal must be able to do several things. It must be large enough to swallow the acorn whole and then dissolve it in its body. Or it must be small enough to make an entrance and devour it from the inside. Or its teeth or its beak must be strong enough to break it into pieces. (Man has machinery to grind it to powder.) Then, no matter what method it uses to take the acorn into the body, the animal must have juices of the right sort to digest it. All the regular feeders manage these. So do many of the others.

Destroyers from the outside

When we think of large animals which are acorn-feeders, perhaps we first think of mammals. About 50 species of wild mammals live on land in Britain. About one quarter of these frequently eat acorns. We would expect the various kinds of rats, mice, voles and squirrels to be among them. Such animals are *rodents*. They have special teeth which allow them to gnaw hard things. Their food is mostly plant matter.

Some of us may know already that there are several sorts of squirrels. Actually, we have four. They are: grey squirrel (*Sciurus carolinensis*), red squirrel (*Sciurus vulgaris*) in figure 13a, dormouse (*Muscardinus avellanarius*), and fat-tailed dormouse (*Glis glis*). In southern Britain, the first is the commonest and the last the rarest. All of them need a great deal of food. After they have eaten their fill, they continue to gather more. What they do not eat immediately, they hide. Some of them put the food in a hollow tree, a hole in the ground, or an old nest. But they are often casual about it. A red squirrel, for example, takes many acorns, even though it lives mostly among conifers. When it hides acorns, it generally runs over the ground and pushes them into the soil anywhere. It may forget where it has put them. The animal does not hibernate (go to sleep in winter). It stays active in all but the coldest weather. Then it discovers some of the buried acorns simply by chance when it searches for food. What does it gain by burying them? Perhaps it hides them from other acorn-feeders which would eat them if they could find them.

Such behaviour is useful to the oak. Acorns have actually been planted and only some of them destroyed. Whole forests of oak can be started in this way. Sherwood Forest, the lair of the great English criminal Robin Hood and his gang, still contains some fine old oaks. Many of these oaks, or their ancestors, were planted by red squirrels. Other oak trees have probably been planted

46

Figure 13. How animals destroy acorns. *From the outside* (pages 46–49): a. red squirrel, b. nuthatch. *From the inside* (pages 49–50): c. *Curculio* weevil and two gall-wasps, d. *Synergus*, e. *Andricus quercus-calicis*. The last seems to be spreading in England.

by jays. Mice and voles, too, store acorns with other fruits and seeds.

And if we can afford it, any of us can pay £10 to plant an oak in Sherwood Forest and receive a charter proving that we own the little plot of land on which it stands.

Some of the mammals which eat acorns may surprise us. One of these is the badger (*Meles meles*). It is related to the fox, stoat, weasel and cat. These are flesh-eaters and their teeth are not particularly suited for dealing with vegetation. But the badger seems to eat almost anything which is not poisonous. It devours acorns as well as other plant material.

A lower proportion of wild birds take acorns regularly. The number is probably around 20 out of 300–400 British species.

The acorn-feeders are varied. Some are game-birds, like the pheasant (*Phasianus colchicus*) and grey partridge (*Perdix perdix*). Pigeons are others. The wood-pigeon (*Columba palumbus*) is one example. All these are adapted for dealing with plant matter. The wood-pigeon is a serious pest. When it can get them, it devours some of the crop plants which man grows for his own use. Sometimes these crops are not available. Then it eats what it can find. Acorns may help to tide it over from one crop to another.

We might expect some of the acorn-eaters to be birds with particularly strong beaks. All the members of the crow family have such beaks. The jay (*Garrulus glandarius*) is one. It takes so many acorns that it receives part of its scientific name from them. *Glandarius* comes from *glans*, an acorn. The jay is a noisy bird with a harsh, chattering voice. And *Garrulus* means such an animal.

During autumn, a single jay can probably gather as many as 5,000 acorns in 10 days. Not all are eaten as they are gathered. The bird hides many of them in storage-places. It may not remember where all the places are. Eventually the forgotten

48

acorns may germinate and new trees develop from some of them. Like the squirrel, the jay helps to establish forests of oak.

Woodpeckers also have strong beaks, but they are not crows. Much of their food consists of insects. But some woodpeckers take acorns, too. A particularly interesting acorn-feeder is the nuthatch (*Sitta europaea*). It is yet another kind of bird with a long, strong bill. It is an acrobatic species which spends much of its time upside down searching for food on trees. The nuthatch has a remarkable way of dealing with hard foods such as acorns (and pieces of chocolate!). It wedges them into a crevice and then hammers away with its bill until they break up (figure 13b). A nuthatch swings from the hips and uses the whole weight of its body as a little sledge-hammer.

Destroyers from the inside

We might expect the kinds of animals which feed inside acorns to include insects. There are numerous species of insects; they are mostly small; and they seem to have invaded almost every sort of situation. Two different groups of insects which sometimes dwell inside acorns are *weevils* (small beetles) and *cynipids* (small wasps).

Weevils are some of our commonest insects. There are many kinds of them. They occur in vegetation of nearly every variety. Most of the oak weevils feed, not inside the acorns, but upon the foliage. But members of one genus—*Curculio*—bore holes in nuts and hard kernels and lay their eggs in the cavity. Acorns are sometimes drilled by species of *Curculio*. They seem to be commonest in the south.

We can tell a weevil from other beetles because it has a sort of snout. If it is one of the nut-boring kind, its snout is used for drilling and is particularly long. But if we find acorns with holes and cut them open and discover grubs inside, they may not be weevil grubs. One way of finding out is to keep some acorns on top of soil in a jar and wait to see what insects appear.

Figure 13c shows one of the *Curculio* weevils which develop from acorns. Another species, closely related to it, lives inside hazel-nuts and is commoner.

Here and there we may find old acorns which have failed to reach full size. They may be distorted, too. Tiny cynipid wasps are one cause. Many cynipids lay eggs on oaks—usually in buds or leaves as we shall see in the next chapter. But two species lay in acorns while these are still very young and soft. Larvae hatching from the eggs take the food which would normally supply the seeds. *Synergus clandestinus* (figure 13d) is the commoner. *Andricus quercus-calicis* is a new insect for Britain, but the ground under some oaks in Devon (Exeter, etc.) becomes littered in autumn with great numbers of acorns it has ruined. There is only one grub in each, and this causes such distortion that the fruit looks like a pyramid with its sides squashed in (figure 13e).

C. THE LEAF-FEEDERS AND BUD-FEEDERS

Where the food comes from

Unlike animals, but like all green plants, an oak-tree manufactures its own food. The *chlorophyll* (green substance) in its leaves traps some of the light rays. Light is one of the forms of energy. With this energy, the oak combines together simple substances taken from the soil and air and makes food. Its leaves are the factories which do this.

Each year, fresh leaves and fresh lengths of twig grow from buds which open in spring. These buds are rich in food ready for the new growth. More animals living on oak get their food from the leaves, the young flowers, or the buds, than from any other parts. They go direct to the source of supply.

Animals which do this behave as members of four groups.

The leaf-feeders and bud-feeders

A. Liquid-feeders. Their mouthparts are like hollow needles. With them, they pierce the leaf and suck the juices.

B. Defoliators. They eat right through the leaf and devour any part of it except, perhaps, the hard veins and leaf-stalk.

C. Leaf-miners. These actually tunnel into the leaf and make galleries (mines). They are so small they fit inside the thickness of the leaf, between the upper and lower surfaces.

D. Gall-causers. Their activities cause the oak to grow and produce swellings (galls). They shelter and feed inside the galls.

Nearly all of these are insects. Probably more than 500 different kinds of insects get their living in various ways from the oak. Those which go for its factories (green parts) cause particular damage. But the reserve forces of the oak are usually equal to this drain.

A. The liquid-feeders

Aphids (greenflies and blackflies) are probably the ones we know best. We may have seen them on poppies and other weeds, or on such crops as beans. There are numerous species which live on many different plants. They are the kinds of insects called *bugs*. Every bug has a hollow beak and takes liquid food. Aphids drink the juices of plants. They can cause damage in two ways. They weaken plants by removing valuable sap, and sometimes by injecting diseases carried on their beaks.

All aphids are tiny. In summer, oak-woods teem with them and their relatives. One of the commonest species on oak-leaves is *Phylloxera quercus*. It is only 1–2 mm long. But even if we do not see the actual insect, we can see its effects (figure 14). It feeds on the underside of the leaf. Its stabs cause little yellow patches to develop and the leaf often arches upwards, too.

Liquid-feeders which are larger than aphids are *capsid bugs*. Again, there are many kinds and they occur on various plants. Some live on oak. Not all capsids feed only on plant juices. A

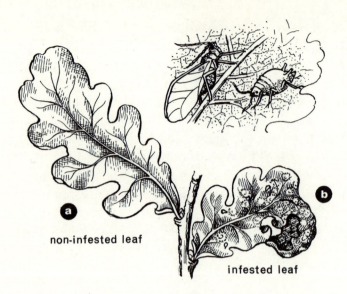

non-infested leaf

infested leaf

Figure 14. Liquid-feeders—effects of aphid *Phylloxera quercus*: a. undamaged leaf, b. damaged leaf.

great many are predators (see page 102) and drink the body-fluids of the animals they attack. Three common capsids which do take some liquid from oak are shown in figure 15.

Harpocera thoracica is the first of the oak capsids to become adult early in the year. It reproduces in May–June. It lays eggs which remain for 11 months and then hatch in the following spring. The young larvae lurk between the scales of the opening buds. They drink sap from the catkins when these come out. Both *Dryophilocoris flaviquadrimaculatus* and *Phylus melanocephalus* feed on the sap in oak-leaves and flowers and also on the juices of little insects like greenflies.

B. *The defoliators*
A few mammals strip oak foliage if they can seize the lower leaves. These include such domestic stock as sheep and goats.

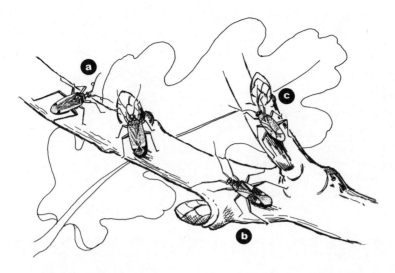

Figure 15. Liquid-feeders—three capsid bugs which drink oak-tree sap: a. *Harpocera*, b. *Dryophilocoris*, c. *Phylus*.

When they get the chance, hungry sheep and goats will browse greenstuffs of almost any sort. Hedgerow oaks are sometimes within their reach.

But these big browsing animals feed on the oak only occasionally. They do far less damage than great numbers of small animals. Some of these always seem to be present on an oak when its leaves are out. Insects are the most noticeable of them. And the most noticeable of the insects which defoliate oak are beetles and moths. There are so many species that we can only mention a few examples here.

Weevils are very common beetles. Some of our most brightly coloured weevils belong to the genus *Phyllobius*. They eat holes in the leaves of trees, especially those of young trees. Oaks are among the species which may be infested.

Much larger than the weevils is the cockchafer (*Melolontha*

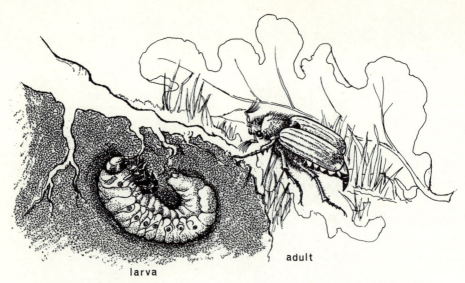

Figure 16. Cockchafer: both defoliator (adult) and root-feeder (larva, page 81).

melolontha). It is a brown insect, nearly 300 mm long (see figure 16). Because it flies in early summer, it is sometimes nicknamed the 'May-bug'. But it is a beetle, not a bug, and has biting mouthparts, not sucking ones. It feeds on the foliage of trees and seems to prefer the oak to anything else. Great numbers of cockchafers are sometimes to be seen at dusk flying around the tops of oaks. They seem to be specially attracted to oaks standing in clearings. When they occur in swarms like this, the damage they can do is frightful. An oak-tree can be completely stripped of all its leaves in a single day! Their larvae live in the soil, where they cause a great deal of damage to roots (see page 81). Fortunately, plagues of cockchafers do not seem to be as common today as they used to be.

As destructive as the cockchafer is the caterpillar of one of the moths. This is the green tortrix or oak-leaf roller (*Tortrix viridana*). The name comes from the caterpillar's habit of rolling up part of the leaf into a cylinder (figure 17). It binds the roll together

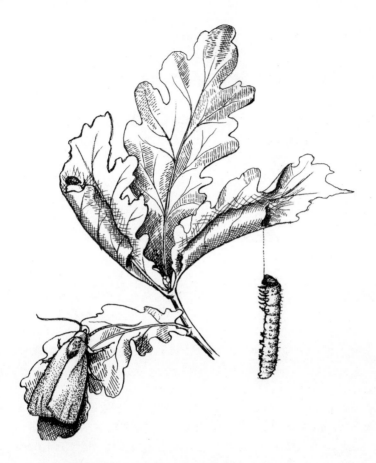

Figure 17. Defoliators: oak-leaf roller.

with silk and shelters inside. If disturbed, it may lower itself from its shelter on a long thread. Although small—up to 11 mm long—the caterpillar is great in its works. An oak-tree can become infested so thickly as to lose all its spring foliage. When this happens, a second crop of leaves may be produced later in the same year.

Other small moths ('micros') occurring in wooded districts, and whose caterpillars eat oak-leaves, include *Phycita spissicella*,

Figure 18. Defoliators—four 'micros': a. *Phycita spissicella*, b. *Acrobasis tumidana*, c. *A. consociella*, d. *Cryptoblabes bistriga*.

Acrobasis tumidana, *A. consociella* and *Cryptoblabes bistriga*. They have no popular English names. Figure 18 gives some of their features. Like the *Tortrix* caterpillar, their larvae shelter in leaves from enemies. *Phycita* and *A. tumidana* are usually solitary. They spin webs and lie concealed in them, each in its own leaf. But many caterpillars of *A. consociella* live socially in a single web, each inside its own silken tube. Several leaves are bound together by the webbing. *Cryptoblabes* occupies a folded leaf. It eats holes between the veins, and then moves to another leaf which it also folds.

Larger moths ('macros'), whose larvae devour the foliage of oak, are numerous. One of the most striking of these larvae is the pale tussock (*Dasychira pudibunda*), shown in plate 10. Many of the moths belong to the group called *geometers*—'earth-measurers'

56

Plate 10. Caterpillar of pale tussock moth (full length, 2·5 cms) on an oak-leaf.

—from the way their caterpillars walk. The caterpillars, nick-named 'loopers', have two separate sets of legs. These are right at the front and back ends of the body. There is a long part between them which is legless. When they move, they draw the rear set of legs up to the front set and arch the middle of the body. Then they straighten out and push the front legs forward to a new position.

Some of these looper caterpillars look astonishingly like twigs, both in shape and colour. No doubt this helps to protect them from predators (see chapter 4f). People often call them 'stick-insects', but the true stick-insects are not native to Britain. Examples of geometer caterpillars, together with the adults into which they turn, are drawn in figure 19.

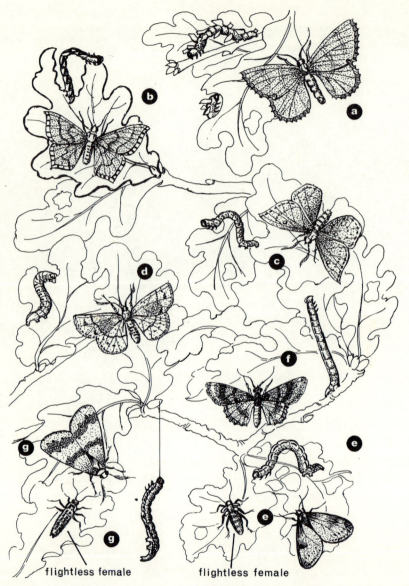

Figure 19. Defoliators—seven geometers: a. blotched emerald,
b. common emerald, c. false mocha, d. maiden's blush, e. winter-
moth, f. red-green carpet, g. mottled umber.

flightless female

flightless female

Several gain extra protection by concealing their bodies in various ways. The caterpillar of the blotched emerald moth (*Comibaena pustulata*) covers itself with fragments of leaf and the scales of buds. Its body has bristles to which these pieces are fixed with silk. When oak-branches are shaken, objects like half-open buds sometimes fall to the ground. After a time, they move and reveal the larvae of the blotched emerald. When it pupates, the larva of the common emerald (*Hemithea aestivaria*) spins a silken cocoon among living leaves on oak-twigs. Both the false mocha (*Cosymbia porata*) and the maiden's-blush (*C. punctaria*) pupate among dead leaves lying on the ground.

Only the male of the winter-moth (*Operophtera brumata*) can actually fly. The female has a heavy body and her wings are very small. The species is a common pest of fruit-trees as well as of oaks. Owners of orchards fasten a sticky band around a tree-trunk to prevent the female crawling up and laying her eggs among the buds. But, when he mates her, the male sometimes lifts her past the band by flying into the air with her. One of the carpet-moths—the red-green carpet (*Chloroclysta siterata*)—takes nectar from the flowers of ivy.

Probably the geometer we are most likely to notice is the mottled umber (*Erannis defoliaria*). Its caterpillars can be as destructive to the spring foliage of oak as those of the green tortrix. The name *defoliaria* is indeed suitable. Again, this is a moth whose female is flightless.

One way of obtaining defoliators is to spread a large sheet (or an open umbrella) on the ground beneath a tree. Then, if the branches are beaten with a stick, small animals become dislodged and fall on to the sheet. The boys in plate 11 are carrying out beating in this way. And many adult moths are attracted by a bright light. These can be caught after dark in a portable *mercury-vapour light-trap* worked from a battery and set up in a clearing. Such a trap is being used in plate 12.

Plate 11. Beating the branches of a tree to dislodge defoliators, etc.

Plate 12. Portable mercury-vapour trap run from a battery. Night-flying insects, attracted by the light, fall through a funnel into a box.

C. The leaf-miners

Weevils, 'micro' moths, and tiny sawflies—insects related to bees and wasps—produce some of the mines we frequently see enclosed in the thickness of oak-leaves. There are various types of these galleries, and we can sometimes recognise the causer by the form of its mine. Five examples are shown in figure 20.

Whatever its shape may be, a mine is the result of an animal devouring the tissues containing chlorophyll from inside the leaf. It avoids the upper and lower surfaces, which have little chlorophyll. A particular mine is usually one or other of two main sorts—a *blister-mine* or a *serpentine-mine*. A blister-mine is formed by a causer which starts to feed in one small cavity inside

61

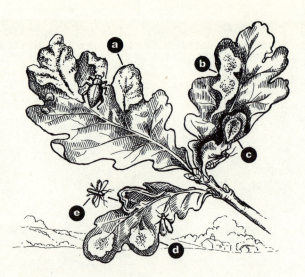

Figure 20. Leaf-miners—five mines: a. weevil *Rhynchaenus*, b. sawfly *Profenusa*, c. 'micro' *Lithocolletis*, d. 'micro' *Tishceria*, e. 'micro' *Nepticula*.

the leaf and then eats this hollow bigger in all directions as it grows. Like Hänsel and Gretel, it gets food from the walls of its house, and it does not travel far to feed. A serpentine-mine is hollowed out by a burrowing animal which travels onwards through the leaf as it feeds. Its gallery gradually widens as it grows, but it never turns round to crawl again along its earlier track.

The larva of the weevil *Rhynchaenus quercus* tunnels a mine which is something like a fan in shape. It starts as a narrow gallery at the *midrib* (the leaf's main vein) and widens out towards the edge. The surface of the blister generally becomes light brown. When it pupates, the insect encloses itself in a ball-shaped cocoon inside the mine.

Profenusa pygmaea is a sawfly whose larva makes a blister-mine rather similar to this. Again, there is a short gallery and then a wide chamber. But the chamber is irregular in shape. Generally it is filled with the brown droppings of the insect. The mine does not extend quite to the edge of the leaf. One which does reach the edge and looks something like the *Profenusa* mine is caused by the caterpillar of the 'micro' moth *Corscium brogniardellum*.

Other caterpillars which make blister-mines include those of the 'micros' *Lithocolletis* and *Tishceria*. There are several species of each. The *Lithocolletis* mine shows as a slight wrinkling of the top surface but looks like a smooth, flattened blister on the underside. The colour is dirty white. *Tishceria* mines are very near the surface and are particularly rounded in outline. They look buff-coloured or yellowish, especially near the middle. There is a silky web inside.

Several species of moths of the genus *Nepticula* have larvae which burrow serpentine mines. These galleries generally run for a time along the leaf-margin before turning inwards towards the centre. They are greyish white and there is a dark line down the middle. The line consists of droppings left behind by the caterpillar as it moves on.

D. The gall-causers

All the animals we have mentioned deform the leaves or flowers in various ways. But the deformities are not galls. A gall only develops if a plant reacts to the injury by *growing*. Usually it grows just around the place where it has been injured. A gall may look very different from the organ which produces it. But every gall grows entirely from the plant's own tissues. Therefore the feeder is not the gall-*maker*. It is the gall-*causer*.

A gall is of benefit to its causer. It provides it both with shelter and a concentrated supply of food. At the same time, the causer is shut off from the rest of the plant, so that any damage it does is isolated.

Probably most plants can produce galls. But they only do so

if they are damaged by the right causers. Those which succeed in causing galls to develop on oaks, for example, generally fail on plants of other kinds. We are not sure how the various causers stimulate their galls to grow.

Oaks are so heavily infested by many different gall-causers that these alone are an important part of 'the world of a tree'. Most of those on oaks are insects. They are so small that we may overlook them. The actual galls they cause are so striking, however, that many of these are easily noticed. It is strange that galls seem to be commoner on scrub oaks (stunted oaks) in hedgerows than on big trees in woods. Part of the explanation may be that causers can reach trees which are in the open more easily.

A gall-causing bug which feeds on the twig itself when this is young and still soft is a *coccid* (scale-insect) named *Asteriolecanium variolosum*. The males have wings and can move about from one place to another. The weird-looking females, on the other hand,

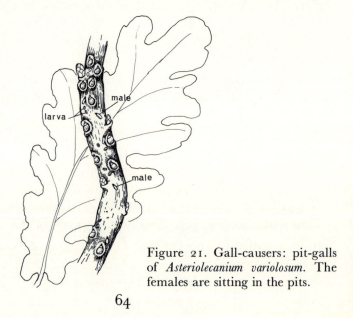

Figure 21. Gall-causers: pit-galls of *Asteriolecanium variolosum*. The females are sitting in the pits.

64

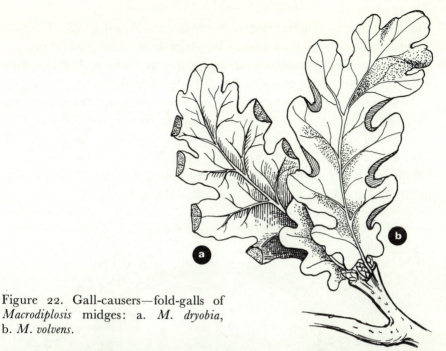

Figure 22. Gall-causers—fold-galls of *Macrodiplosis* midges: a. *M. dryobia*, b. *M. volvens*.

have neither wings nor legs and cannot move. They scarcely look like animals at all. Each remains fixed for life in one spot on the twig. Here she feeds by sucking sap. A little wall, about 1 mm high, grows around her. Soon she is lying in an oval pit gall measuring about 2 × 3 mm. These pits generally contain feeding insects from May to October. Years later, long after the coccids have died, we can still find empty galls on old twigs. Figure 21 shows some of the features of this unusual gall.

Sometimes we see an oak-leaf with a fold at the edge. If the fold has grown thick and is not held together by silk, it is likely to be the work of a *gall-midge* called *Macrodiplosis*. Two species are fairly common and we can tell their galls apart. The one caused by *M. dryobia* lies at the *end* of a leaf-vein and folds towards the *lower* surface. A gall caused by *M. volvens* lies *between* two veins and folds towards the *upper* surface. Figure 22 shows

65

the differences. The overlap in both cases is about 4 mm. Usually several maggots live in each fold—these are the midge larvae. After a time, the maggots fall out and enter the soil. Here they become pupae and, eventually, adult gall-midges.

Nearly all the galls on oaks which are easily noticed are due to *gall-wasps* (cynipids). More cynipid species occur on oaks than other plants. In Britain, there are roughly 30 species of oak cynipids. About half of them are rare. We can expect to come across nearly 20 kinds in most districts in the south. Some occur in the far north, also.

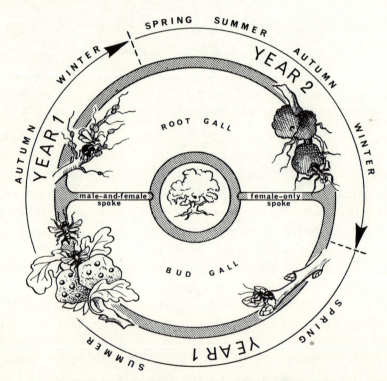

Figure 23. Gall-causers: how the life-cycle of the gall-wasp *Biorhiza pallida* is like a wheel with two spokes (page 67).

Many of the oak cynipids have a remarkable life-history. There are two generations of adults in it. One is entirely a female generation. At this time, there are no males. The females lay eggs in exposed parts of the tree, such as buds, flowers or leaves. Even though there are no males to fertilize them, these eggs actually hatch. The larvae which emerge from them feed on the tissues of the oak inside galls which they cause to develop. When they are fully grown, the larvae pupate inside their galls and turn into adults. What comes out of these galls is a generation of adults of two sexes. This time there are males as well as females. The males mate with the females and die shortly afterwards. Then the mated females lay fertilized eggs in a part of the oak where they are likely to be protected in some way during the winter. Occasionally this is the root. These fertilized eggs hatch into larvae and here, again, galls are formed. Months—even years—later, the larvae become adults and leave their galls. And all these adults are females. They are the females which make their way to the exposed parts and lay unfertilized eggs there.

We probably find this hard to understand at first. But the diagram in figure 23 should help us. The cycle is like a wheel with two spokes. One is the female-only spoke. The other is the male-and-female spoke. As the wheel turns, one spoke follows the other round.

If we take some actual cases, we can see what really happens. In this book, we only have room for about half a dozen common examples.

1. Oak-apple (*Biorhiza pallida*). The apple-gall, which is common on twigs in early summer, is caused by larvae hatching from unfertilized eggs. At the end of winter, the female lays these eggs in a bud. By June, the gall has become a round lump, buff and pink in colour, and 3–4 cms across. It feels rather soft and spongy, not hard and woody. If we find one which is brown

67

and very hard, it is a different sort of gall altogether (see no. 2).

The apple-gall is the *male-and-female* spoke. Around midsummer, both sexes emerge in large numbers from apple-galls. They look something like brown flying ants. They bite their way out through separate small holes. By collecting apple-galls when they are mature (large and pinkish, but without holes), we can keep them in jars until the insects appear. If we put blotting-paper and a little dry sand in the bottom (see figure 24), moisture is absorbed and the galls should not go mouldy. If they do, we should use a stiff brush to remove the mould as soon as we notice it.

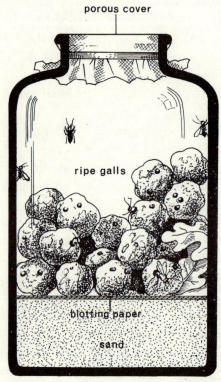

porous cover

ripe galls

blotting paper

sand

Figure 24. Gall-causers: jar for rearing insects from galls.

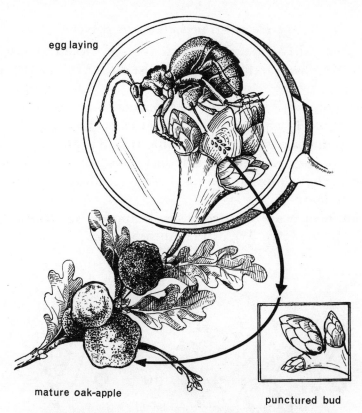

egg laying

mature oak-apple

punctured bud

Figure 25. Gall-causers: wingless female of *Biorhiza pallida* laying unfertilized eggs in a bud (page 70). Her young cause the bud to form an oak-apple.

We may be amazed at the great numbers of insects which come out of them. Not only the actual causers themselves, but other species appear, too. Some of these are 'gate-crashers' which moved into the gall after it had formed and made use of its tissues for food. Others kill and eat the causers or some of the gate-crashers.

The males and females mate. Then the mated females fly down to the soil and burrow underground. Here they lay fertilized eggs in the roots of the oak. Larvae which hatch from these eggs cause root-galls to develop. Each root-gall looks like a small potato. If we wish to find one, we must dig for it, like the boy in figure 31.

The root-gall is the *female-only* spoke. Females emerge after two winters. They have no wings. They leave the soil in February, climb up the oak-trunk, and lay unfertilized eggs in buds on the twigs. Apple-galls then develop here instead of leafy shoots. Figure 25 shows this happening. Look back also to figure 23 and ahead to figure 32.

Many people are puzzled by galls and do not really understand what they are. We can try this catch on our friends.

Figure 26. Gall-causers—the two galls of *Andricus kollari*: a. female-only gall (oak marble) on common oak, b. male-and-female gall on Turkey oak.

Question—'What is the fruit of the apple-tree?'

Answer—'The apple'.

Question—'What is the fruit of the oak-tree?'

Answer—How many of them reply, 'The oak-apple'?

2. Oak-marble (*Andricus kollari*). People sometimes mistake this gall for the last (oak-apple). But this one is dark brown, round, woody and very hard. The name, oak-marble, is suitable. Nowadays it is one of the commonest cynipid galls in Britain. But it is not a British native. It was introduced nearly 150 years ago, when galls were brought into Devon from abroad. A great deal of tannic acid could be extracted from them by breaking them up and soaking the pieces in water. The acid was used for making ink or dyeing cloth. Evidently some of the cynipids escaped before the galls had been destroyed in this way. These insects were able to set up galls on British oaks. The species spread rapidly from Devon and now occurs in most parts of the country. In the last century, people became worried about its spread. They were afraid that it might ruin the acorn-crop.

There is a single grub inside each marble-gall, instead of a large number as in the oak-apple. Naturalists who have gathered marble-galls and reared them have always found that the only causers which emerge are females. In other words, the marble-gall is the female-only spoke in the life-cycle.

Where is the gall of the male-and-female generation?

We shall be lucky to find it. We need to search among the buds of a different tree altogether—the Turkey oak. Here we may come upon little oval galls which remind us of the ants' 'eggs' sold in pet shops for feeding fish. (They are really the ants' cocoons, not eggs.) The galls are not very noticeable and they may be high up. Males and females emerge from them in the summer. After mating, the females lay fertilized eggs in the buds of common oaks and the hard, woody, marble-galls develop as a result and survive the winter. Both galls are shown in figure 26.

Andricus kollari is a strange insect. Very likely its life-cycle is changing. If there are no Turkey oaks in a district, it seems able to do without the male-and-female stage altogether. The un-mated females can fly. They simply move to other common oaks and lay their unfertilized eggs in the buds. When they do this, marble-galls develop which are exactly like the ones from which the females came. And more females come from these, but no males.

How is the marble-gall protected? It does not form under-ground, like the root-gall of *Biorhiza*, but high on a twig. Perhaps its hard wall is an advantage against cold and damp. But birds like woodpeckers, which have strong beaks, often attack it to reach the juicy grub inside.

3. Oak-artichoke (*Andricus fecundator*). Oak cynipids include several different species of *Andricus*. This one has a life-history which is more 'ordinary' than the last.

Its female-only generation, corresponding to the marble-gall insect, also develops in a bud. A female which has been mated lays a fertilized egg in a bud on a twig. This happens more commonly on oak-bushes than on large trees. The larva which hatches causes the bud to grow into a gall. Generally this starts to develop in June. In due course it look like a green-and-russet artichoke. Usually it is about 2 cm long. Unlike a real artichoke, it is tough and hard. There is a solid core inside on which the growing larva feeds. Eventually the larva becomes a flying adult female. She may leave the gall in the spring after she was laid, or two or three years later.

When the time comes for her to lay eggs, these are unfertilized. She lays them in the flower-buds which produce the male catkins. She seems to prefer the pedunculate oak to the sessile oak. The pedunculate is the earlier of the two species to come into flower. Perhaps this is the reason.

Hairy catkin-galls grow where she has placed her eggs. Each

72

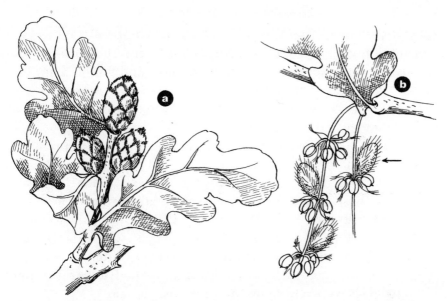

Figure 27. Gall-causers—the two galls of *Andricus fecundator*: a. female-only gall (oak-artichoke), b. male-and-female gall (hairy catkin-gall).

of these galls is only about 3 mm long. They form little swellings along the catkin stalk. Out of them come the male-and-female generation, and these insects appear in May or June. After mating, the females lay the fertilized eggs which start the development of the artichoke-galls. Figure 27 gives the two galls.

Again, there is a gall which needs to survive the winter—perhaps several winters—in an exposed position on the oak. Again, the fact that the gall is a thick, solid structure may help it to do so.

4. Red-barnacle gall (*Andricus testaceipes*). Very few galls form actually on the roots of oak. *Biorhiza pallida* protects its female-only generation in this way (see no. 1). So does *Andricus quercus-radicis*, whose female-only stage develops in truffle-galls on the upper parts of the roots near the base of the trunk.

Most oak cynipids have a female-only generation which needs

73

special protection because part of its development takes place during winter. Both *Andricus kollari* (no. 2) and *A. fecundator* (no. 3) enclose this stage in galls which are hard and tough. They can survive the cold even high up in bare trees. A commoner sort of protection is for galls to become covered with a blanket of *litter* (dead leaves).

This is what happens in *A. testaceipes*. In August or September, its mated females lay their fertilized eggs. They insert them very low down near the ground in rows into twigs. Such twigs are generally those springing up from small oak-shrubs in a hedge. When the eggs hatch, the larvae from them cause galls to form. As they develop, these galls push their way through the surface of the twig. At first they are red and soft, but later brown and hard. They are about 6 mm high and shaped something like the barnacles we see attached to rocks by the sea.

As time passes, autumn leaves drift into the hedge and cover them. This is why they are easily overlooked. They can be present in almost any overgrown hedgerow containing oak-shrubs. But we may have to move thick piles of litter to find them.

Barnacle-galls are not mature before April of their third year. Then they fall from the twigs. Only female causers emerge from them. These lay unfertilized eggs in the main vein or stalk of the young oak-leaf. Leaf-vein galls develop here: these are simply green swellings. By the autumn, the leaf-vein galls are mature and insects of both sexes escape from them. After mating, the females produce the fertilized eggs which give rise to the barnacle-galls.

Look at figure 28.

5. Oak-cherry (*Cynips quercus-folii*). Several oak cynipids gain protection by their galls falling to the ground and then becoming covered with litter. One of the largest galls to which this happens is the oak-cherry.

Figure 28. Gall-causers—the two galls of *Andricus testaceipes*: a. female-only gall (red-barnacle gall), b. male-and-female gall (leaf-vein gall).

If we find it, we are likely to be impressed. It is a brightly coloured sphere, 2 cms across, attached to one of the veins. It forms on the underside of the leaf and there may be several on one oak-leaf. The causer is a larva developing from a fertilized egg. Therefore it will grow into an adult female. There is a single grub in each gall.

During autumn, the larva becomes fully grown. Then it turns into a pupa inside its gall. By this time, the gall has fallen from the tree. As it lies on the ground, a thick covering of dead foliage falls on top of it. In this way it remains protected from hard weather. It may also be hidden from some of its enemies, such as birds.

Although the females leave their *pupae* in October, they wait inside their *galls* until weather conditions are favourable. They escape finally in late winter, around February. Their unfertilized eggs are laid in buds on small twigs. As they develop, the larvae cause the buds to grow into violet-egg galls. Each of these is

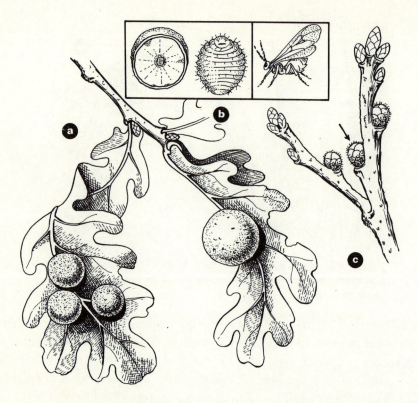

Figure 29. Gall-causers—the two galls of *Cynips quercus-folii*: a. female-only gall (oak-cherry), b. grub and adult wasp from oak-cherry, c. male-and-female gall (violet-egg gall).

about 3 mm long and contains one insect. Such galls are not particularly noticeable. But they are purplish in colour and have a velvety look, and show up clearly in strong sunlight. They grow in April–May, adults of both sexes emerge in June, and fertilized eggs are immediately inserted in the leaf-veins.

Cherry-galls arise where these eggs have been laid. Figure 29 includes some of the features of the insect and its galls.

6. Oak-leaf spangles (*Neuroterus*). Many of us know these small discs on the underside of leaves without realizing what they

are. Years ago, people thought they were parasitic *plants* feeding on the juices in the leaves. Actually, they are galls containing the female-only generation of cynipid wasps. There is a single larva inside each of them.

A spangle-gall is attached to its leaf by a tiny stalk. In autumn, the stalks snap and the spangles fall to the ground. About a fortnight later, the leaves follow and cover them. The litter seems to be essential for the insects to survive. Probably there are three main reasons for this.

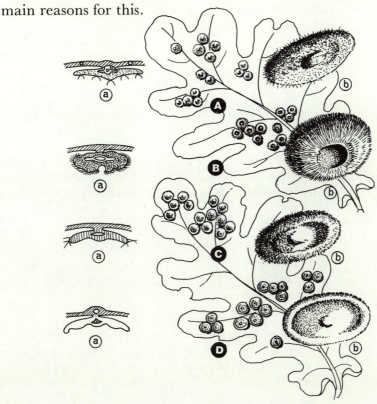

Figure 30. Gall-causers: spangles of *Neuroterus*—section (a), surface-view (b). A. *Neuroterus quercus—baccarum*, B. *N. numismalis*, C. *N. tricolor*, D. *N. albipes*.

1. In winter, it tends to be warmer under the litter than in the open.

2. Even though they are separated from the tree, the galls continue to expand. They do so by absorbing water. If they dry up, the grubs inside soon die. Experiments show that the litter helps to keep the spangles damp.

3. Great numbers of spangles lying on the ground are devoured by game-birds (pheasants, etc.). Leaf-litter makes it harder for such enemies to find them.

GALLS OF *NEUROTERUS* SPECIES

Species	Female-only Gall (Autumn–Winter)	Male-and-Female Gall (Spring–Summer)
N. quercus-baccarum.	Common spangle. Flat, reddish green disc, 6 mm across, with hairs like stars.	Currant gall. Like red currant, 4 mm across, in male catkins.
N. numismalis.	Silk-button spangle. Thick, golden brown disc, 3 mm across, with hollow in middle and covered with glossy hairs.	Blister gall. Like blister, 3 mm across, in leaf.
N. tricolor.	Cupped spangle. Greenish yellow, hairy disc, 3 mm across, with rim raised up.	Hairy-pea gall. Hairy sphere, 6 mm across, on underside of leaf-veins.
N. albipes.	Smooth spangle. Cream-coloured saucer, 4 mm across, without hairs.	Schenck's gall. Oval green body, 2 mm long, in recess on edge of leaf.

The root-feeders

Four species of *Neuroterus* cause spangles on British oaks. All are fairly common. In some districts, we may find three or even four kinds on the same leaf! If we wish to rear the spangles we must keep them moist. One way is to enclose them in a plastic bag with a wad of damp cotton-wool. Another way is to put them in a jar with a small dish of water by their side.

The adult females come out of their spangles in spring. There are no males at this stage. These females are the mothers of the male-and-female generation. Depending on the species, they lay their unfertilized eggs in the catkins or various parts of the young foliage. Galls develop here out of which the two sexes emerge in summer. After mating, fertilized eggs are inserted in the leaves and cause the spangles.

The table on page 78 and the drawings in figure 30 will help us to identify the four sets of galls.

D. THE ROOT-FEEDERS

The search

By using an implement with a narrow blade, we can dig as far as the upper roots of an oak-tree without disturbing the ground too much. A fern-trowel (figure 31) is one suitable tool. We may have to search for a long time before we come upon any root-feeding animals. We are groping in the dark. All the same, we have something to guide us. Scientists have found that under-ground animals live near the surface. They are in the topsoil, where rotting leaves enrich it and hold moisture. This applies to those moving freely in the soil. It is also true of animals which take food from roots.

Plants use their roots for support as well as feeding. An oak-tree is so heavy that its roots spread wide. But they rarely go deeper than two metres. It must be a well-balanced tree with its *centre of gravity* low down. Its wide roots are more likely than its

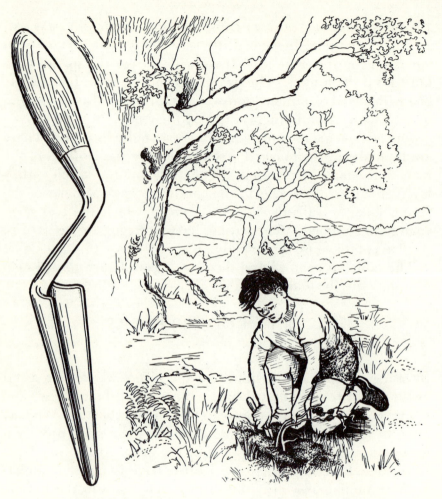

Figure 31. Fern-trowel for uncovering tree-roots in topsoil.

deep ones to have animals. We may have to dig far beyond the tree's *axis* (main trunk) to reach them.

Many of the animals mentioned in the last chapter depend completely on the oak for food. If oaks disappeared the animals, too, would die out. Few of those which devour oak-roots are as dependent as this. Most can feed on the roots of other plants. They eat the roots of herbs (plants with soft stems) as well as those of woody plants (shrubs and trees).

Animals which can eat oak-roots

Two examples are, the larva of the cockchafer beetle and the caterpillar of the common swift moth (*Hepialus lupulina*).

We know already that the cockchafer is a defoliator of oak (page 53). Its larva is even worse as a pest. This eats roots, not leaves. It can bite through the roots of oaks—especially those of young trees—and cause harm. But it is more destructive still to the fine roots of grasses and corn-crops. It works its way through the soil slowly. No doubt it can easily find quantities of grass-roots close together, whereas oak-roots are more spread out.

During its feeding, the larva becomes a fat white grub with a brownish head. Farmers sometimes call it the 'rookworm'. It is eaten in great numbers by rooks, whose beaks are long enough to reach it. Evidently its own diet is not very nourishing. It takes three or four years to grow from the egg into the adult beetle! Cockchafer swarms (see page 54) come in cycles. These are every three or four years, too, and depend on the time the grubs take to develop. Figure 16 includes a drawing of the grub.

There are five British species of moths called 'swifts'. Their caterpillars all feed on the underground parts of plants. These are mostly herbs, with roots just below the surface, like bracken and grasses. However, the common swift eats a variety of roots. Sometimes it devours those of oaks. It bites holes in the new, soft growths—the parts where the trees are taking up water.

Older roots are too hard and woody. Seedling oaks, or small trees in hedges, are damaged from time to time.

Animals which must eat oak-roots

Oak cynipids which cause galls to appear on the roots are more closely linked with the tree than these. They cannot bring about the formation of galls on anything else. We stand a fair chance of finding the root-galls (female-only generation) both of *Biorhiza pallida* (see below) and *Andricus quercus-radicis* by digging near oaks whose shoots have been galled by the male-and-female generation. We may even find the root-galls of a third cynipid—*Andricus rhizomae*—but this is unlikely, because it is a rare insect in Britain.

We can decide whether a particular swelling on an oak-root is probably a gall caused by a cynipid wasp simply by cutting it open. An egg, grub, or chrysalis inside is more likely to be a stage in the life-cycle of a gall-wasp than anything. We need to bear in mind that the actual insect we see may be something which attacks the true gall-causer. Or it may be a gate-crasher feeding on the tissues of a gall already caused by a cynipid. If we study the drawings in figure 32, we should be able to distinguish between the root-galls caused by the three species.

In all of them, the galls have no stalk and sit directly on the root. The females of all three emerge from the galls in their second winter.

Biorhiza pallida develops on main roots and also on small rootlets. The galls are more or less spherical in shape and about 8 mm across. They occur in clusters and several individual galls may stick together and merge. If we cut one open, we shall find it contains a single cavity with one insect inside. At first the colour is pink, but it darkens through red to dirty brown with age. By the time they are mature, the galls look like tiny old potatoes.

82

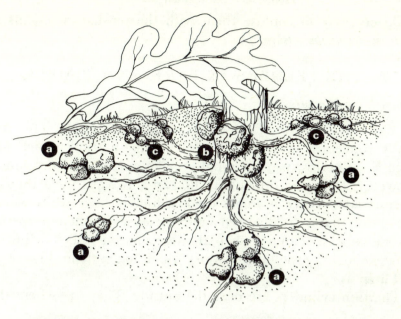

Figure 32. Root-feeders—three root-galls caused by gall-wasps:
a. *Biorhiza pallida*, b. *Andricus quercus-radicis*, c. *A. rhizomae*.

Root-galls of *Andricus quercus-radicis* (truffle-galls) are larger and between 3 and 6 cm across. They develop on the roots of young trees, especially those which are 2–5 years old. Unlike the *Biorhiza* galls they contain several cavities, with one insect in each. They start by being cream in colour. As they mature, they develop a reddish-brown tint. The surface is often split, so that they look like fruits which have been partly peeled.

The male-and-female generation develops in little galls in a young twig or a leaf-stalk.

Galls of the rare *Andricus rhizomae* are smaller than either. Again they occur on trees between 2 and 5 years old. Generally they are very near the surface and may even be on roots which are exposed. They are like little cones with the tips cut off and have ridges along the sides. They are grouped in clusters. But

83

it is very easy to confuse them with the red-barnacle-galls of *Andricus testaceipes* (page 73).

E. THE FEEDERS IN BARK AND TIMBER

Where the food occurs

An oak-trunk consists of several different *zones* (layers). They are really concentric cylinders. If we examine a trunk which has been sawn across, we can usually make out most of the zones. However, some are difficult to find in this way. Even though their circumference is huge, these cylinders have walls which are so thin that we really need a microscope to see them properly. All the same, we can tell whereabouts such thin-walled cylinders are if we identify the thicker zones which touch them. Figure 33 will help us.

The thin cylinders are near the outside. They are where the

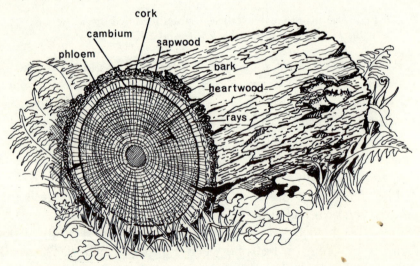

Figure 33. Some of the parts of an oak-stem. The *cork* cambium lies between the phloem and the cork. Fungi which destroy the heartwood (see plate 16) may enter by cracks along the rays.

84

trunk is growing wider. Not all the trunk is growing. Indeed, most of it (heartwood) is dead. The dead part is usually dry. Even though it is dead, it is still useful to the tree. It helps to support it—just as beams made from heartwood help to support a building.

Parts of the outer zones are alive. They are also damp. In the warmer months there is considerable activity here. Water is travelling upwards in the sapwood from the roots to the leaves. Food is travelling downwards in the phloem from the leaves to the roots, and is being stored in places. Two very thin layers—the cambium and cork cambium—are adding fresh growths. The cambium is making more sapwood and phloem. The cork cambium is making cork and filling up gaps in the bark. Both these cambium cylinders need food. They are growing actively and causing the trunk to increase in width. By examining a sawn trunk we can calculate its age by counting the number of *annual rings* laid down in the wood by the cambium year after year.

Perhaps it is not surprising that some animals should feed on the outer layers. They are reached more easily than the deeper ones and there is more nourishment in some of them. Even after they have died, nourishment remains for a considerable time in these outer parts.

The large animals

Quite large animals sometimes seek food from the trunks of oaks. Generally they go for sapling trees before the bark has become too thick for them to bite through. They include such animals as squirrels and voles and—in hard winters—rabbits. Bucks (young males) of the roe-deer (*Capreolus capreolus*) damage trees by rubbing their growing antlers against the trunks. The friction removes the 'velvet' covering the horns.

When animals bite deep into the bark all the way round in a

circle, their activities can cause serious injury. This sort of damage is called *ringing* the trunk. If they cut through the phloem, the food supply to the lower parts is interrupted. If they go deeper still, into the sapwood, the water supply to the leaves is affected. There may be enough food stored in the parts near the ground for buds below the ring to open. If there is no further destruction, the buds may grow into leafy branches. But the central trunk and its crown of branches die away. Such an oak ceases to be a normal tree and becomes a shrub. We often see oak-shrubs in a hedge. Here their shape has probably been caused by human beings cutting the stems when building the hedge.

The makers of shallow tunnels

We are likely to notice the work of small animals which feed on the oak more frequently than these large ones do. Beetles, for instance, are often plentiful inside both living and dead trees. The most obvious effects are mainly caused by *bark-beetles*. These make complicated galleries in the cambium, just underneath the bark. The galleries become noticeable through the bark peeling off. It often does this at places where the insects have been at work. Sometimes the beetles excavate in the rough posts of oak-fences, and the same thing happens here.

The elm bark-beetle (*Scolytus scolytus*) seems to be the species whose galleries are best known. It is very common and harmful, and it destroys many elm-trees every year. It occurs on the oak and on trees of several other kinds, too. Here it does less harm. Another gallery-maker, the oak bark-beetle (*S. intricatus*), is also found on trees of various species. But in this case the oak is the chief one.

We can make out something of what happens during a beetle's tunnelling operations by examining an old gallery.

When the oak bark-beetle is about to reproduce, one male and one female come together on the trunk or bough. The actual

86

tunnelling is the work of the female. She gnaws a hole in the bark. Both insects pass through this hole and reach the growing parts underneath. Here the male hollows out a *nuptial chamber* and the two beetles mate in it. When she is ready to lay, the female bites out a long *egg-gallery* under the bark. This is a corridor which runs horizontally from the nuptial chamber, so that it cuts *across* the fibres passing up-and-down the trunk. Eggs are laid in the walls of this corridor. When they hatch, the larvae make their own galleries at right-angles to their mother's, so that these larval passages run *with* the fibres. As a result, the tunnels together form a pattern something like the skeleton of a fish. Figure 34 and plate 13 show what we can see. While biting its way through the tissues, each larva feeds on the sugars, starches, etc. it meets. Eventually it becomes fully grown. Then it widens the end of its burrow to form a small chamber. It becomes a pupa here and then an adult beetle.

After making the nuptial chamber, the only work the male does is to push out the tiny wood chips caused by the tunnelling.

But the directions of the galleries really seem to have very little to do with the direction of the wood-fibres. Probably they have more to do with the direction of gravity. Look again at plate 13. Here the beetles pierced the bark of an oak-trunk as it lay on the ground shortly after being felled. Its fibres ran the wrong way. All the same, the egg-gallery was still tunnelled horizontally and the larvae still made their galleries up-and-down.

Other species excavate galleries which are slightly different. All bark-beetles are more or less cylindrical and very small. Their shape is well adapted for tunnelling into wood. Often it is easier to identify a species from the kind of gallery it makes than by examining the actual insect.

The larvae of some kinds of beetle which penetrate the bark feed mostly on a fungus growing in the galleries. These are

87

ambrosia-beetles. To the Ancient Greeks and Romans, 'ambrosia' was the mysterious food eaten only by the gods. Perhaps naturalists who first watched these insects feeding thought there was something mysterious about their food, too. Having no chlorophyll, and being in the dark anyhow, the fungus cannot make its own food. Instead it gets its nourishment from the gallery walls, the woods chips from the tunnelling, or the manure from the larvae. When it is present, the walls are nearly always stained dark brown or black.

Eventually, the fungus becomes bulky, like the mould on jam or stale bread. Its *spores* (reproductive bodies) are brought into the galleries by the beetles themselves. We are not sure whether the beetles bring them in deliberately or by chance. It rather looks as though it might be deliberate, because a particular species of fungus often grows in the tunnels of a particular species of beetle. The two seem to be closely associated. If this is true, then the beetles set up a sort of kitchen-garden inside their habitat. They grow a crop for their own use. But it is a crop which can prove fatal. Unless it is grazed frequently enough, the fungus blocks up the narrow galleries. If this happens, the beetles inside gradually die off.

Many ambrosia-beetles tunnel deeper than the bark-beetles and penetrate into the wood itself. Their galleries vary, and the shapes of two are compared in figures 34b and c. Both are tunnelled in the moist sapwood. The larvae of neither species excavate channels. They feed on ambrosia and the juices of the tree.

Xyleborus xylographus occurs in southern England. It lives in oak and in several other kinds of trees. Its egg-gallery is irregular in shape and ends in a flattened, shallow chamber. The general direction is horizontal. *Anisandrus dispar* is found in trees of many species, but chiefly in oak. Its borings consist of a horizontal main gallery with short branches. They are the work of the

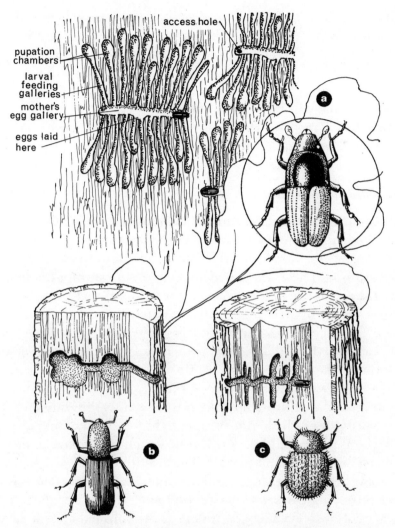

access hole

pupation
chambers

larval
feeding
galleries

mother's
egg gallery

eggs laid
here

a

b

c

Figure 34. Feeders in bark and timber—galleries of bark-beetles and their allies: a. oak bark-beetle (*Scolytus intricatus*), b. ambrosia beetle *Xyleborus xylographus*, c. ambrosia beetle *Anisandrus dispar* (male, female shown in gallery is more cylindrical). The leaf indicates sizes of the insects, not their galleries.

89

female. A third species, *Trypodendron domesticum*, whose galleries are not shown, tunnels in oak and beech.

We can tell whether the beetles are active by examining the little round entrance on the outside of the trunk leading to their hidden gallery. If they are doing their boring, some kind of powdery dust will be present. The male will have pushed it out. If the dust is nearly white the beetle is a wood-borer, such as *Xyleborus*, *Anisandrus* and *Trypodendron*. If it is brown the insect is a bark-borer, like *Scolytus*.

The makers of deep tunnels

Many more beetles come to the trunks of oaks. Some feed on liquid oozing from wounds in living trees. Others penetrate right inside the wood, either of trees which are still alive or of dead stumps. Three kinds which occur in the stumps of old oaks sometimes appear indoors. When they do, all three can become serious pests by feeding inside wooden beams or furniture. These are, the death-watch beetle (*Xestobium rufovillosum*) and two furniture-beetles, *Anobium punctatum* and *Ptilinus pectinicornis*. A fourth, the powder-post beetle (*Lyctus fuscus*), has a larva which burrows in living sapwood only.

Larvae tunnelling deep into timber cause the damage. The wood provides so little nourishment that they take several years to develop into adult beetles. Death-watch beetle larvae usually feed in old roofs made of oak. Their activities are worst where the roofs become wet from time to time. *Anobium punctatum* is the most annoying furniture-beetle we have. It lays its eggs on the surface of wood which is rough (not polished). The larvae ('woodworms') then bite their way inside. A piece of furniture can collapse completely if many of these larvae infest it. The powder-post beetle must lay its eggs in wood with large pores, such as oak. Its larvae make a fine powdery dust, whereas the dust from *Anobium* and *Ptilinus* holes is coarse and grainy.

It is difficult to rid our buildings of these pests for long. There are reservoirs of them out of doors living in the stumps of oaks and other trees. With the decline in oak-trees, some are taking more and more to human dwellings. *Anobium punctatum*, for one, is gradually increasing in numbers as a household nuisance.

A much larger insect than these breeds in oak-stumps. This is the stag-beetle (*Lucanus cervus*). If we see either the adults or their larvae, we shall be impressed. An adult male can be 5 cm long and a female only slightly less than this. It is one of the biggest beetles in Europe. Although it occurs in many parts of southern England, we are most likely to find it in the Home Counties, near London. Fortunately, it does not attack furniture or building-timber! Despite its startling appearance, it is harmless.

Its larva burrows far into the rotting wood of old stumps. The food is so poor that the insect takes three years or more to become adult. Furthermore, the nourishment varies a good deal from one stump to another. Adult stag-beetles vary a good deal in size, depending on the quality of the food they received as larvae.

'Stag-beetle' is named from the male's fierce-looking mandibles (jaws). They are branched, something like the antlers of a male deer. Actually, the beetle does not bite with them. It uses them when displaying to the female before mating. Observers have sometimes noticed flying males grasping the twigs of oak-trees with them when alighting from mid-air. The female's mandibles are small in comparison, but she can bite.

A close relative, the lesser stag-beetle (*Dorcus parallelopipedus*), is found more often in rotting stumps of beech than oak.

Beetles are not the only insects whose larvae devour wood. Two moths—the goat (*Cossus cossus*) and the leopard (*Zeuzera pyrina*)—feed as caterpillars inside the branches and trunks of oak. They make cavities inside trees of several other species as well.

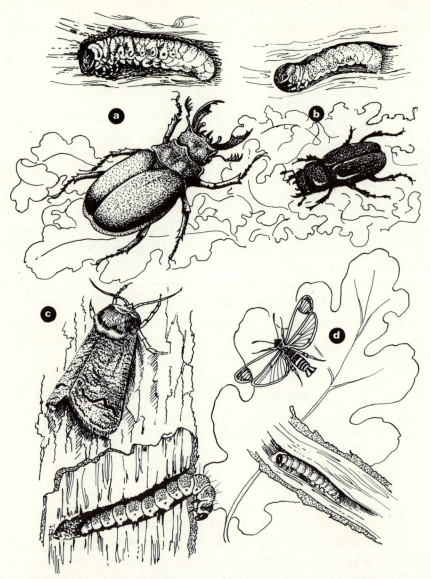

Figure 35. Feeders in timber—insects which make deep tunnels: a. stag-beetle, b. lesser stag-beetle, c. goat-moth, d. yellow-legged clearwing moth.

Like some of the other timber-feeders, both have long life-histories. They live inside the wood, completely hidden from view, for three years or more.

All the same, we are more likely to notice the caterpillar of the goat-moth than the moth itself. When it is fully grown, after several years, it becomes restless. It leaves its hole and wanders about in the open searching for somewhere to pupate. It is a pale caterpillar, as long and thick as a man's little finger. Its sides are pink, its back is red, and it has a strong pair of mandibles with which it bites its way through the wood. Eventually it goes underground and pupates in a cocoon of soil-crumbs bound together with silk. (The leopard-moth larva pupates inside its burrow and makes a cocoon of wood-particles and silk.) An

Plate 13. Tunnellings of *Scolytus* beetles underneath bark of fallen oak-trunk lying horizontally. The egg-gallery remains in the horizontal plane but runs parallel with the wood-fibres instead of across them. Length of egg-gallery, 4·5 cm.

Plate 14. *Corylopsis* bush with pieces bitten out by leaf-cutter bees. The fragments were used for the cells in plate 15.

Plate 15. Tunnels made by beetle larvae and lined with foliage by leaf-cutter bees.

adult goat-moth is the colour of oak-bark. When it is at rest on a tree-trunk, it is easily overlooked.

The name 'goat-moth' really comes from the caterpillar. It smells something like a billy-goat.

A strange little moth, which looks more like a wasp than an ordinary moth, also breeds in oak-stems. This is the yellow-legged clearwing (*Aegeria vespiformis*). Its caterpillar feeds just underneath the bark and seems to prefer the stumps of newly felled trees. Although it occurs in many parts of southern England, it is not easy to find.

Some of these timber-feeders are drawn in figure 35, and the damage done by beetles appears in plate 13. And plates 14 and 15 show what can happen after the tunnellers have left. Other animals sometimes move in as shelterers and take over. A kind of small bee—the rose-leaf cutter (*Megachile willughbiella*) is one example of the group—has done this in the photographs. It has constructed little cells from semicircular pieces bitten out of thin foliage, and here its own young are reared.

The makers of the largest cavities

Trunks and branches of oaks can become so hollow that any wood still left is merely a thin wall enclosing the cavity. In plate 16, the boy is examining a slice through an oak-bough 75 cm across, which is in this condition.

Eventually part of the wall may collapse of its own accord and reveal the hollow. Or an affected bough may look sound

Plate 16. Section through a huge bough of an ancient oak hollowed out by rot-fungus. Compare its size with the 13-year-old boy.

enough from the outside and then suddenly break away when pressure is applied. This is one of the risks in climbing trees.

Nearly always, the damage is caused by fungi (see page 127) and not by animals. Several different fungi bring about rot of this kind. They are able to destroy the actual walls of the cells forming the heartwood, even though nourishment is low here. There are two main groups. Those fungi which destroy the walls while these are still young and soft and cause *brown rot* of timber. And a second group which make use of walls which are older and harder and cause *white rot*.

F. THE ATTACKERS

The two main kinds

In this chapter we are concerned with animals which attack other living animals and obtain food from them in some way. Most of the victims are herbivores feeding on the oak. Therefore the attackers, too, depend on the oak for food, even though they do not eat it directly. The attackers include both predators and parasites.

Predators are animals which attack, kill and eat other animals —their *prey*. Parasites can be animals or plants. They feed on other things—their *hosts*—while these are still alive. Usually an animal which is a parasite soon dies if its host dies. But certain plants which are parasites change their feeding habits so that they survive by taking nourishment from the dead body (see page 127). As we shall find out, it is sometimes difficult to decide whether an animal is really a parasite or a predator.

The predators

We might expect predatory animals to be powerful, like foxes, badgers, stoats and weasels. Or we might expect them to be particularly active, like the long-eared bat (*Plecotus auritus*), which flits over the crowns of oaks and picks off flies, moths and beetles resting on the leaves. But few of them are really large. Those we notice most readily, however, are such active animals as birds. Many species either live in oak-woods or appear there from time to time. One which is well adapted for oak-wood conditions is the blue-tit (*Parus caeruleus*).

If we put out food in our gardens for birds during hard weather, the blue-tit is likely to be one of the most regular visitors to the supply. At such times it is not a predator. Indeed, much of the food we provide is probably vegetable (kitchen scraps, bread, nuts, and so forth). Plant matter may be sufficient to tide a fully grown blue-tit over the winter. Nevertheless, it becomes a predator if it can find small animals. The period in its life-history when the animals are particularly important is in summer, when it has young to feed. Growing birds need the prey for meat (protein) to build up their bodies.

Its victims include spiders, great numbers of aphids, plant bugs of other kinds, the young and adults of weevils and beetles, moth-caterpillars, fly-maggots, the larvae of gall-wasps, and even such animals as millipedes which lurk inside crevices. Except for the spiders—which themselves are predators—most of these invertebrates are herbivores. All of them are kinds which are abundant where there are oaks. And hollows in the oak-timber may be suitable as nesting-sites.

A blue-tit has a *territory*—an area near its nest from which it gets its food. Various things affect the size of the territory. One of these is the spacing of oak-trees. Where they are close together, the territory is compact and small. Where they are widely separated, it is bigger.

Most of the other small birds in oak-woods are predators, too. Among them are, the robin (*Erithacus rubecula*), hedge-sparrow (*Prunella modularis*), tree-creeper (*Certhia familiaris*), and the leaf-warblers—the chiffchaff (*Phylloscopus collybita*) and wood-warbler

(*Ph. sibilatrix*) are two of these. During summer, all take great quantities of little invertebrates—or the eggs of invertebrates—which feed where there are oak-trees. In turn, the small birds are attacked by larger vertebrate predators. The sparrowhawk (*Accipiter nisus*) is such a predator. It picks off its victims by suddenly darting at them from behind the cover of trees.

The owls mentioned on page 36 are predators and take the occasional bird. But most of their prey consists of plant-eating mammals and large beetles. Magpies and carrion crows are more serious. They devour many eggs of other birds.

Predators accounting for the destruction of the greatest number of small animals are small themselves. For example, the numbers of aphids and other invertebrates taken in a single day by a blue-tit are greater than the numbers of birds taken by a sparrow-hawk. Most of the predators on oak-feeding invertebrates are themselves invertebrates. There are many species. Together, they kill and devour far more of the little herbivores than do the larger predators.

Aphids (greenflies) seem particularly to be the prey. In fact, we can regard them as the starting-point for many of the animals which feed on meat. Five groups of invertebrates—all of them insects—are examples of the kinds of things which obtain food from aphids. These are, lacewing-flies, hover-flies, capsid bugs, ladybird-beetles and ants. They are shown in figure 36. We will consider them separately.

A. Lacewings

All are exceptionally dainty-looking insects with straight wings like delicate gauze. Even if they do not know what they are, people are often impressed when they see them. Fourteen of the 60 British species are fairly large.

Lacewings have feeble powers of flight and movement, so that their prey needs to be something which itself is rather inactive.

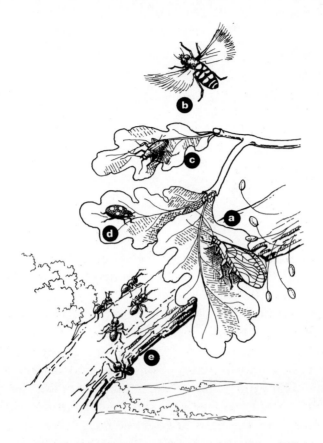

Figure 36. Predators—adults of five insects which obtain food from aphids: a. lacewing, b. hover-fly, c. capsid bug, d. ladybird, e. ant.

Usually, this means aphids. The adult lacewings chew up the aphids' bodies. The larvae, however, have sucking mouthparts. They drink the body-juices of the aphids without any solid matter passing into their mouths.

A female lacewing lays her eggs on a plant stem. When doing so, she first touches the stem with her abdomen and fixes to it a tiny drop of liquid. She raises her body and draws out this liquid which solidifies in the air. Then she expels the egg. As a result, each egg is attached to the tip of a fine stalk. Whole clusters of these stalked eggs are set together.

Probably the habit is a protection against such enemies as ants. Larvae of some species of lacewings entangle the skins of their sucked-out prey among the spines which cover their own bodies. In this way, they build up a protective shield which hides them from other enemies.

B. Hover-flies (syrphids)

We are probably familiar with some of these beautiful insects. There are numerous species. All look something like wasps or bees. But each has a single pair of wings instead of the two pairs of most insects. In fact, they are related to houseflies and blue-bottles and not to wasps and bees.

Adult syrphids are generally common in summer in the clearings and path-ways inside oak-woods. Here we may notice them in the warm sunshine hovering in mid-air in one position and then suddenly darting to one side and hovering in a new position. The adults may take nectar or pollen from flowers, but their larvae have feeding habits of three different kinds.

Some dwell in the nests of bees or wasps. Here they eat waste matter (droppings, etc.) coming from the grubs developing in the cells. The owners of the nests tolerate them. No doubt they are useful as scavengers and help to clean up the interiors.

Others live in the dung of vertebrates, or in rotting plant matter, or in foul water (see figure 10c). Again, such larvae feed on waste material.

None of these are predators.

The third type are predators on aphids. They are rather strange in appearance and look something like small leeches. They are flat along the underside.

There are places inside oak-woods for larvae of all three types.

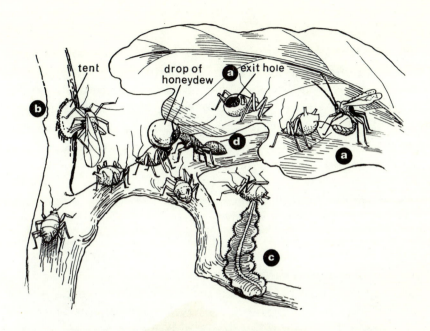

tent

drop of
honeydew

exit hole

Figure 37. How four insects obtain food from aphids: a. *Aphidius*
(page 108), b. *Praon* (page 109), c. hover-fly larva (page 100),
d. red-ant taking honeydew (page 103).

An aphid-eating larva deals with its prey in a curious manner.
The female hover-fly lays her eggs on foliage where there are
aphids. When it hatches, the larva is only about 2 mm long. It is
totally blind and finds its victims by chance as it waves its head
from side to side. When it makes contact with the aphid, it
plunges its mouthparts into the body. Then it raises its head
and holds up the prey away from the leaf on which it had been
feeding. The predator gives the impression of a performing seal
balancing a ball on its nose (see figure 37c). Then it sucks the
body dry and casts the empty husk aside. It kills about four
aphids on its first day. By the time it is 10 days old, and fully
grown, its food consumption has increased so much that it may
be destroying as many as 120 aphids in a single hour!

C. Capsid bugs

A capsid, being a true bug, always takes liquid food of some kind. Its mouthparts are hollow and pointed like a sharp beak. They can pierce plant tissues and be used for extracting sap, or they can pierce animal tissues and be used for extracting body fluids. We have considered plant-feeding types on page 51. Here we are concerned with those which are predators.

Many capsids are predators at some time in their lives. Common species which occur on oak, and take particularly the juices of aphids, include *Phytocoris reuteri*, *Megacoelum infusum* and *Miris striatus*. A fourth, *Calocoris quadripunctatus*, is unusual in one way. Its growing larvae feed mainly on the unripe catkins of oak. But the full-grown adults take food apparently richer in body-building protein and suck aphids' fluids.

Most of the predatory capsids seem to attack almost anything small. *Phytocoris tiliae*, another species common on oak-trees, sucks caterpillars, red-mite spiders, and even the pupae of lady-bird beetles—insects which are also predators on aphids. *Cyllecoris histrionicus* includes in its food the female-only larvae of cynipids causing spangle-galls on oak-leaves. It pierces the gall with its beak to reach its prey inside.

The last two capsids attack aphids, too.

D. Ladybird beetles (coccinellids)

As is well known, these pretty little beetles are great destroyers of aphids. Ladybirds feed on aphids both during the larval and adult periods of their lives. They differ from most of the insect predators we have considered already. Instead of sucking liquids from their prey, they chew up their bodies.

The female beetle lays her eggs on a leaf infested with aphids. They hatch in eight days and the larval period lasts about three weeks. Many hundreds of aphids are devoured by a single larva in this time. Then it pupates. The pupa is stuck to the leaf and not concealed in any way, and the beetle emerges in a week or so. Destruction of aphids is continued by this adult.

Although some predatory birds take coccinellids, they do not seem to be eaten very much by them. Perhaps they find them distasteful. The insects are strongly marked or brightly coloured and are particularly noticeable. Furthermore, they do not hide but feed in the open. Sometimes they cluster together so that they become still more noticeable. In this way, they may advertise themselves, and their colour may give warning that they are unfit to eat.

E. Ants

Several species of ants are generally common near oak-trees. Two which occur particularly in woods are the jet-ant (*Lasius fuliginosus*) and wood-ant (*Formica rufa*). The jet-ant often nests in rotten stumps and the wood-ant builds mounds on the woodland floor. A third species, the red-ant (*Myrmica rubra*), establishes its nests in a great variety of places. Red-ants are often to be found in decaying wood, at the bases of oak-trunks, and running up and down the trees themselves.

Many people know that some ants have a special relationship with aphids. Ants take a mixed diet but they are mostly predatory. They kill a great range of invertebrates, from caterpillars to other ants. They may obtain food from aphids, however, without killing them. What they extract from them is really a sort of waste matter (excretion) called *honeydew*. It is a sticky substance which we notice for ourselves on the leaves of oaks and other trees in summer.

Aphids—and also some other insects related to them—produce honeydew when they are feeding on plant sap rich in nourishment. The honeydew itself is highly nutritious. A single large aphid can produce up to 1·7 cu mm of honeydew in one hour. A colony of jet-ants can obtain about 8 kgs of honeydew from aphids in 100 days. An ant collects the honeydew by stroking the hind end of the aphid with its antennae until a droplet appears (figure 37d). At once the ant sucks it up and moves on to another aphid for more. If there are no ants around, the aphid still produces its drops of honeydew. But it kicks them away with its last pair of legs. Honeydew discarded in this way is what causes the stickiness of summer foliage.

Biologists who have made a special study of the subject have discovered that honeydew is important for ants. Those which are able to get it fare better than those which are unable to do so. Their colonies become larger and reproduce more success-fully. This happens even when there is no shortage of other food. Evidently honeydew supplies nourishment of a kind which is difficult to come by in other ways.

Certainly ants are much attracted by aphids and may under-take considerable journeys to reach them. Red-ants, for instance, visit over 50 species of aphids and sometimes go 100 metres to obtain honeydew from them. These travels are guided by a special sort of navigation. Jet-ants lay down scent trails to places where aphids are numerous, and other ants probably do the same. We may come upon columns of ants moving like two-way traffic up and down the trunks of oaks. It is interesting to trace them to the aphids in one direction and to their nest in another.

Sometimes ants carry aphids' eggs to their nests and look after them here. Aphids are often to be found living in the nests. And the jet-ant has been seen to put out aphids of one species to 'graze' on oak-trees. But some ants kill aphids and bring their bodies back to the nest. Presumably they are then eaten. Some of the stories about ants tending herds of aphids like cattle, and building special shelters for them, are probably exaggerated.

Predatory birds—woodpeckers and the robin are examples—feed on ants. A stranger relationship is when birds pick up living ants and push them in among their feathers. Ants defend themselves by spraying poison (formic acid) into the air when they are disturbed. Birds use ants as a source of insecticide. The formic acid helps to kill irritating parasites (feather-lice) in the plumage.

General predators from the invertebrates are so varied that we can mention only a few of them.

Spiders, which are very numerous indeed, are probably some of the most important. They capture flying insects of almost any kind. Scorpion-flies are a particular feature of shady places like oak-woods. They, too, take a wide range of small insects; but most insects they kill are ones which are already sickly or injured.

Many of the predators are beetles. Rove-beetles (*Staphylinidae* =

Plate 17. Open wood with mixed trees, decayed timber, and sunny rides, in a sheltered valley far inland. Many oakwood organisms occur here. *Malvern.*

Plate 18. Animal traps on oakwood floor. Pitfall trap is in the middle, loose bark is near the handforks, and fruit-rinds are being laid down.

'staphs') abound where they can reach suitable prey. One of the commonest is *Philonthus politus*, a shiny black insect with brassy wing-cases. It lives in mosses, fungi, animal dung, the decaying remains of dead vertebrates, and so forth. Here it hunts for fly larvae. Another common staph, *Quedius assimilis*, also lives in moss and also takes maggots. Where woods are open and sunny (like that in plate 17) we may find one of the most impressive of all staphs, the devil's coach-horse (*Ocypus olens*). Usually it hides under moss and scraps of fallen wood and other waste. It seizes a variety of prey and hunts in the open more than most beetles of its kind. When disturbed, it adopts a threatening attitude by lifting the rear of its body upwards and forwards and opening its mandibles.

Rove-beetles, and other small animals which wander over the ground, are easily collected. They tend to gather under flat pieces of bark or inside grapefruit husks laid on the soil. And they fall into a jar sunk below the surface, particularly if such a *pitfall-trap* is fitted with a slippery funnel. These collecting methods are being used by the boy in plate 18.

Clerids are beetles of another group. They are useful because their larvae attack the grubs of wood-boring beetles and bark-beetles.

We have already considered capsid bugs (pages 51–2 and 102). Whether these drink plant sap or animal juices, we probably think of them as insects dwelling among foliage. A few, however, live elsewhere. *Xylocoris cursitans* is one which spends most of its time under the bark of fallen and rotting boughs of oak. It is a predator on other small invertebrates living in the same place— tiny thrips, springtails, and the larvae of several sorts of beetles.

What we have examined so far are things we can easily see. This applies even to cases where the predators are little invertebrates. But some attackers are so small that they are able to feed inside the bodies of their victims while these are still living.

They are parasites and the victims are their hosts. Where the hosts are small, such internal parasites are so small that we can easily overlook them. We may come across them at certain times —for example, when they have completed their feeding and are ready to disperse.

The parasites

Those associated with oak which we are most likely to find in this way are insects. Some are parasites inside animals' bodies. Many—not all—belong to the great insect order called the *Hymenoptera* (ants, bees, wasps, etc.). Their hosts are insects, too.

Such parasites have astonishing features. Two of them are:

1. The small size of some of their hosts;

2. The fact that the parasites may be attacked by other parasites (hyperparasites) and these, in turn, by parasites of their own (hyper-hyperparasites).

Parasites on aphids illustrate both these features. A common example is seen when we find lifeless aphids, with the skin hard and brownish. On some, there is a clean-cut round hole at the end of the abdomen with a sort of circular lid hinged nearby. This is the work of a tiny *braconid* named *Aphidius*. (Braconids are one group of parasitic hymenopterans.) *Aphidius*, barely 2 mm long, looks something like a very tiny wasp (figure 37a). It has developed from an egg inserted through the skin of the living aphid by the female braconid. While it was a larva, and growing, it fed on its little host's body-fluids but did not destroy the vital organs. By continuing to feed, the aphid provided its parasite with a continuous supply of nourishment. Then, on becoming adult and having no need for further food, the braconid killed its host and left the dead body through the little trapdoor.

Sometimes the escape-hole has jagged edges. This reveals that the braconid, when full-fed, was attacked through the aphid skin by a hyperparasite. In this case the hyperparasite is a *chalcid-wasp*, a still smaller hymenopteran. Having fed on the juices of the braconid, it killed it and emerged by making a hole with irregular margins in the husk of the aphid. And even this is not the end of the story. The chalcid may be attacked, and eventually killed, by a third species, a hyper-hyperparasite!

Over two centuries ago the writer Jonathan Swift wrote a neat verse about a situation of this kind.

> So, naturalists observe, a flea
> Hath smaller fleas that on him prey;
> And these have smaller fleas to bite 'em,
> And so proceed *ad infinitum*.

We are unlikely to notice the work of *Aphidius* readily because it leaves little evidence. Another braconid called *Praon*, which also attacks aphids, is more noticeable. It is no bigger than *Aphidius*, but it abandons the aphid it has killed while it is still a larva. Instead of cutting its way through the tip of the abdomen, the larva emerges through the lower side. Then it spins a cocoon like a sloping tent with a broad base and narrow top. The base is fixed to the leaf and the aphid's dead husk is stuck to the top of the tent. *Praon* pupates inside the tent and the adult braconid emerges from it. One of these tents is included in figure 37b.

Although they are small, the tents show up clearly on the leaves of oak and other trees. Again the braconid has a parasite—a chalcid named *Pachycrepis*.

Much larger hosts than aphids are attacked by braconids or other parasitic hymenopterans. For example, the braconid *Microgaster alvearius* lays eggs inside some of the looper caterpillars which are common on oaks and other trees in woods and hedgerows. Like *Praon*, the parasite kills its host and leaves the dead body while still a larva. But in this case a huge number—fifty or more—may emerge from a single caterpillar. They spin their cocoons just outside its body. The larvae that issue first

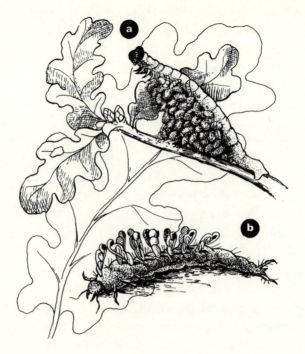

Figure 38. Insect larvae killed by parasites: a. wall of *Microgaster* cocoons underneath looper caterpillar, b. pupae of *Proctotrypes* on devil's coach-horse larva.

from the dying host make the lowest cocoons. These are attached to the support where the caterpillar is clinging. Those emerging later spin the highest cocoons on top of this foundation just under the arch of the caterpillar's looped body. As a result, a remarkably regular and solid-looking wall is built up from cocoons stuck firmly together (figure 38a). The adult insects emerge through circular doors bitten in the flanks of the cocoons.

When fifty larvae issue from one caterpillar, does this mean that the mother braconid jabbed her victim fifty separate times and laid one egg on each occasion? Or did she make one jab and lay them in a cluster, all at the same time?

Actually, there is a third possibility. So strange are certain of these insects that one egg can give rise to a single embryo which then divides into several embryos. This state of affairs is *polyembryony* (*polys* = many, *embryon* = young). Polyembryony accounts for some of the cases. It is almost certainly the way by which the tiny hymenopteran, *Proctotrypes niger*, is able to produce more than twenty offspring out of a single larva of the devil's coach-horse beetle (page 107). The dead host can sometimes be found lying on the ground with the *Proctotrypes* pupae standing on their tails and jerking up and down (figure 38b). Generally there are two to each segment of the host's body in which they had lived as larvae.

The ways in which the parasites introduce their eggs vary. Sometimes they are laid on the skin of the host and the larvae make their way inside. More commonly they are inserted into the host's body by the mother's *ovipositor* (sting). Even when they are deeply hidden, many insects become hosts of these killer-parasites. For example, the caterpillar of the goat-moth (page 93) which lives inside the wood of trees, has its parasite. This is yet another kind of hymenopteran—an *ichneumon*—named *Lissonota setosa*. Its body is 4 cm long, and half of the length is the ovipositor. This slender, hollow needle can be pushed into the timber until it reaches the caterpillar—which the ichneumon cannot even see! *Lissonota* stings the caterpillar but passes eggs into its body instead of poison. The stung caterpillar is doomed.

Such cases are merely examples. Enormous numbers of the invertebrates associated with oak suffer this fate. And many of the parasites are flies, not hymenopterans. We should try to decide what is really happening.

Usually the relationship between a parasite and its host is so nicely balanced that the two live together indefinitely. Here the

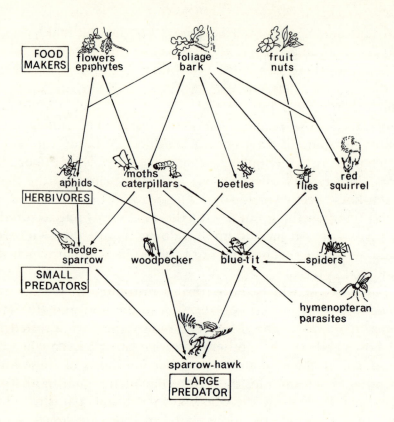

Figure 39. Part of the food-web linking a few of the organisms inside an oak-wood. The arrows show which way the food flows.

situation is different. The victims are feeding for the sole benefit of their attackers. For a time they remain alive and the attackers receive a continuous supply of food from them. Then, as soon as the attackers have finished feeding and are ready to disperse, the victims die. They never reach maturity.

What are these attackers, really? Are they true parasites? Or are they predators which 'budget well'?

Whatever it may eat, every animal really depends on green plants for its food. Even if it is a predator which eats other predators, the prey, in turn, feeds on herbivores which obtain food from plants. Food is passed from one organism to another along a *food-chain*. More accurately, it is a *food-web*, since there are many branches connecting the living things together. Food-webs are complicated in detail but simple in principle. Their origin is always green plants—the world's food-factories.

Figure 39 represents part of the food-web linking organisms associated with oaks.

Some oakwood herbivores obtain their food, not from oak-trees directly, but from other plants which depend on oaks. All these plants are part of 'the world of a tree'.

5. How plants use the oak

The variety

So far we have ranged from man to small insects. Apart from the oak itself, rot-fungi (page 96), and the ambrosia eaten by the young of some beetles (page 88), we have concentrated on animals.

Rot-fungi and ambrosia-fungi are plants. But they contain no chlorophyll. This means that they cannot use sunlight to make their own food. They have to feed on material supplied by the oak or by something which has eaten the oak. Nevertheless many of the plants which use the oak do have chlorophyll. Such plants depend on the tree in various ways. Some use it as a surface on which to grow. Others use it as a support for climbing. One may get part of its nourishment from the tree and manufacture part itself. Another may need the particular kind of shelter the oak provides.

We may be able to understand some of these features if we consider actual examples.

Plants with chlorophyll

Probably we already know by sight the commonest green plant growing on the surface of oak-trees. It is so common we often take it for granted. We overlook it and forget that it is there.

Yet it must be one of the commonest kinds of green plant in Britain!

This is the green powder which grows on the trunks and branches of oaks and many other trees. It rubs off so easily that grown-ups may complain if we climb trees in our best school shorts. Although there are no roots, stems or leaves, it shows up from a distance. This is because it consists of enormous numbers of plants growing close together.

We need a microscope to make out the plants separately. If we have a chance of examining the powder in this way, we shall see that each plant is a tiny, bright green sphere. Its scientific name, *Pleurococcus*, means 'flank-berry'—that is, the ball (berry) which grows on the side (flank) of something. We can find it on the sides of many different things—trees and shrubs, fences, bricks, walls of stone or concrete, and even the glass panes in a greenhouse. Such variety shows that it cannot be very closely associated with the oak.

By examining the situations where *Pleurococcus* lives, perhaps we can work out for ourselves some of the conditions it needs. If we visit an oak-wood, we may find it on the trees all round the edge but not on those right inside the wood. We may find it thick on the west side of a solitary oak growing in the open and thin on the other sides. Prevailing winds are usually from the west, so that rain is driven on to the trunk from this direction. Furthermore, the west is lit by the sun without becoming very hot and dry. And if we watch the streams of water running down the trunk during a rainstorm, we may notice that the plant misses these but grows along their edges.

Evidently, *Pleurococcus* needs a surface wetted by rain but where water does not flow in a torrent. It also needs light but cannot survive where the hot sun dries the surroundings too much. The surface of an oak-tree is merely one of many which commonly provide the necessary conditions.

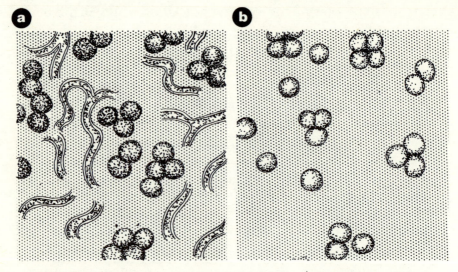

Figure 40. Microscopic epiphytes from oak-trunk (page 117): a. lichen (algal cells + fungal hyphae) from dry side, b. unmixed alga from damp side. Each sphere is 0·025 mm in diameter.

Very often the situation is more complicated than this. We may find some of the powder all round the tree. Even without the use of a microscope, we notice differences in its appearance from one side to another. Where the surface stays cool and damp, the powder looks light green and smooth. Where conditions become hot and dry, it has a greyish or yellowish tint. It is also split up into little areas by fine cracks.

A microscope shows other differences. The greyish or yellowish material has little hairs among the green plants. The hairs branch and make an untidy network. They are hollow and are really branched tubes. They have no chlorophyll, so that they are not green. The green colour is in the little spherical plants. These green spheres are the bodies of an *alga*. But the branching tubes are the body of a *fungus*. Most fungi are made up of hollow tubes. The tubes are called *hyphae*. These, then, are the hyphae of a fungus. Where an alga and a fungus are mixed up together like this, what is formed is a *lichen*. Comparisons are given in figure 40.

In drier parts, therefore—perhaps on the east or south sides— we find lichens. These greyish or yellowish coatings are *crustaceous lichens* (=powder lichens). It is impossible to remove them from a surface without breaking them up.

How do they survive where it is dry? The two plants in a lichen are partners. One helps the other. The alga is kept damp by moisture held between the hyphae, while the hyphae get some of the food made by the alga.

We may notice lichens of other kinds, too: flat lichens which lie close against the bark and are roughly circular. These are

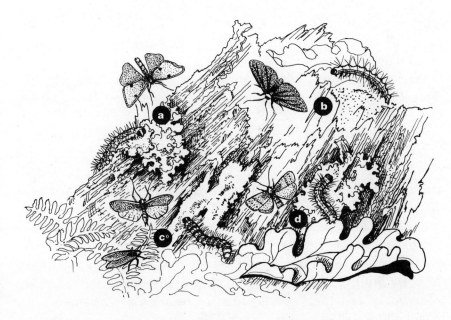

Figure 41. Epiphytes—footmen moth and their lichen-feeding cater- pillars (page 118): a. red-necked footman, b. rosy footman, c. four- dotted footman, d. common footman.

foliose lichens (=leafy lichens). Or we may see some growing in tufts attached to the tree by a little stalk—*fruticose lichens* (=tassel lichens). Both leafy and tassel lichens are fairly easily removed without damage. Powder and leafy lichens occur widely, but tassel lichens seem to be rare in districts where the atmosphere is polluted by smoke, etc. We are likely to find all three groups on the same tree in suitable localities—near the sea in western areas, for instance.

Quite large caterpillars eat some of the oak-tree lichens. They are not defoliators, like those on pages 54–9. The chief ones are the larvae of footmen moths. Figure 41 shows four of the commonest—red-necked footman (*Atolmis rubricollis*), rosy footman (*Miltochrista miniata*), four-dotted footman (*Cybosia mesomella*) and common footman (*Eilema lurideola*). When the moths are at rest, they fold their wings closely along the body and then look very stiff. This probably accounts for the name 'footmen'. They stand like servants on duty.

When algae and lichens grow upon trees, they merely live there but do not feed on them. They are *epiphytes* (*epi*=upon, *phyton*=plant). Oaks carry many epiphytes. Some, like liverworts and mosses, are bigger plants than algae or powder lichens.

About a dozen species of mosses and four of liverworts are common epiphytes on oak-trees. Usually they live where conditions are wet and shaded. Thus, they tend to be low down near the roots of living trees and on the fallen boughs and rotting stumps of dead ones. We need to consult a reference-book to distinguish the various species. But we can generally tell liverworts from mosses. Liverworts are of two main kinds. Either they lie horizontally, and have no stems or leaves but are made up of green lobes which overlap; or they have upright stems with leaves. The second—leafy liverworts—have leaves which look flattened and are in two rows on opposite sides of the stem. Mosses have shoots which look bushy and their leaves are in a

Plate 19. Extracting animals from epiphytes by enclosing the vegetation in a muslin bag and immersing this in a funnel of warm water.

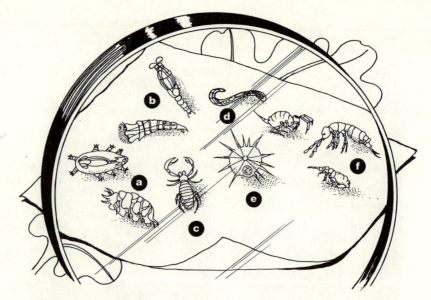

Figure 42. Epiphytes—six kinds of animals extracted from mosses (plate 19): a. water-bears (tardigrades), b. rotifers, c. false scorpion, d. eelworm, e. protozoan, f. springtails (collembolans).

close spiral up the stem. Leafy liverworts are the sort of liverworts we are most likely to find on oak-trees.

All these epiphytes—algae, lichens, liverworts and mosses—often provide spaces (microhabitats) for tiny animals. The animals may be hard to pick out simply by searching through the plants. One way of finding them is to do what the boys are doing in plate 19. They have gathered epiphytes from oak and enclosed them in a cloth bag. Then they have immersed the bag in water held in a funnel. They are illuminating and warming the water by an electric-light bulb above the funnel. Animals driven from the plant material by this treatment escape through the pores of the bag and collect in the stem of the funnel. They can be obtained by opening the clip. Figure 42 shows some of those extracted from epiphytic mosses.

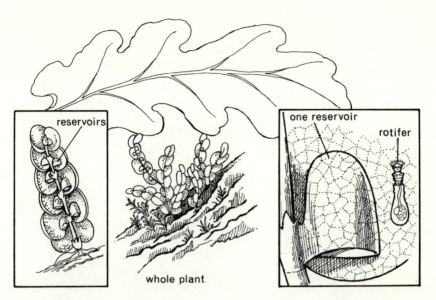

Figure 43. A microhabitat: the liverwort *Frullania dilatata* and its special rotifer *Callidina symbiotica*. The leaf indicates the size of the whole liverwort plant.

Sometimes a particular epiphyte has a particular animal associated with it. One example is the leafy liverwort *Frullania dilatata*. It is common around the base of oak-trees. Its name, *dilatata*, refers to its leaves. They are *dilated* (swollen) so that water collects in them. Perhaps they act as reservoirs which help the liverwort to survive dry periods. If we examine the liquid from them under a microscope, we may find a tiny water animal living there—a *rotifer* of the particular species *Callidina symbiotica*. So closely linked is the animal with the small reservoirs that we are unlikely to find it anywhere else. Both the liverwort and its rotifer are given in figure 43.

Where the climate is wet, some of the mosses, at least, grow high up the trees. They extend along the boughs and trap particles of soil between their shoots. Again these epiphytic mosses are not

Figure 44. Epiphytes: common polypody fern on oak-bough (plate 24).

necessarily alone. They may provide a hold for still larger plants.

One example of a large epiphyte which can live in such situations is a fern, the common polypody (*Polypodium vulgare*). It is easy to recognise (figure 44). Its fronds have rather broad, straight leaflets with smooth edges. There may be spore-cases on the undersides in orange clusters. It has a short, thick stem which lies horizontally. This can penetrate small crevices and then enlarge to take up the shapes of the holes. Numerous roots grow from the stem and work their way among the mosses and into spaces in the rough bark. Thus, the fern becomes securely anchored. Numbers of polypodies sometimes festoon the mossy boughs of a single oak.

Figure 45. Epiphytes: herbs and shrubs growing in hollow near top of oak-trunk. The plants would not come into flower all at the same time.

Even flowering plants grow as epiphytes in such places as the forks of boughs, or where branches have been cut off so that a hollow crown is left. Dead leaves and a little soil gradually collect here. The plants which move in are very varied. They include such kinds as willowherbs, whose seeds float in the wind. We may also find bushes of hawthorn, dog-rose, rock-spray (*Coton-*

easter), and even gooseberry (figure 45). All these plants have fruits which are eaten by birds. Have birds brought them?

And the large epiphytes can provide habitats for smaller things. We may find algae or lichens attached to the twigs of the bushes. Here are epiphytes growing on other epiphytes, in fact.

No epiphytes are rooted in the soil in which the oak is growing. They take all they need either from the air or from matter on the surface of the tree. Therefore, climbing plants such as ivy (*Hedera helix*), whose stems often grow thickly over the trunks and boughs of trees, are not really epiphytes. The main part of their root-system is in the ground. Their shoots eventually die if they are cut off from it. Indeed, one way of destroying ivy is to saw through the base of its stem close to the soil.

Ivy-covered oaks are commoner in the open than deep inside woods. We often see them in hedges. Ivy can stand a certain amount of shade, but not too much.

When ivy grows over living trees, it uses them mainly for support. It cannot be closely associated with them, because it grows just as successfully over things which are not alive—walls and ruined buildings, for example. At the same time, it may get some nourishment from its supports. It holds on to them with small roots growing from its branches. If we tear a branch away, the roots break off and remain clinging to the support. Some water may be absorbed through these roots while they are joined to the ivy branch. Even after all connections with the soil-roots have been cut, branches sometimes continue to live for months.

Does ivy seriously damage a living tree over which it climbs? No one is sure of the answer. Its leaves might cut down the light reaching the tree's foliage. It might take matter out of the ground which the tree could use. Ivy-stems often become thick and woody, and these might compress a tree so that its growth is hampered. Ivy certainly causes damage to buildings. It keeps them damp. It penetrates crevices in brickwork and widens them.

But if we find a dead oak-tree clad in ivy, this does not mean that the ivy killed it. Many stumps killed by other means become covered in ivy before they finally break up.

Ivy is used as a nesting place by birds of several species. One is the stock-dove (*Columba oenas*). Usually it occupies holes, including those in old timber. Sometimes it breeds behind ivy covering hollows in trees. Sometimes the actual ivy-branches form hollows it can use. Wood-pigeons and stock-doves eat ivy-berries, and slugs, snails and insects shelter in its foliage. And, in autumn, insects gather nectar from its flowers.

Few of our native climbing plants cling to their supports as firmly as the ivy. When honeysuckle (*Lonicera periclymenum*) climbs up a tree, it twists its own stems together and makes a 'rope'. When the rope becomes woody, this alone provides much of the support. Old-man's-beard (*Clematis vitalba*) merely loops its leaf-stalks around projecting twigs and then hangs down.

A fairly large plant which is more closely associated with trees is the mistletoe (*Viscum album*). It is a parasite. Although it is green and makes food, it needs something from a living tree. It penetrates deep into the tree's wood. Perhaps it gets water and minerals in this way. Whatever mistletoe does obtain, the tree must be alive. Even the particular branch on which it is growing must be alive: if it dies, the mistletoe dies also.

Mistletoe grows on trees of different kinds. If we ask our friends to name some of them we are likely to hear the oak mentioned. Often it is the very first to be mentioned. Many people immediately think of oak when they think of mistletoe.

But the truth is that mistletoe on oak is very rare indeed. So rare is it that, if we notice mistletoe growing on a tree whose name we do not know, we can be practically certain that it is not an oak. Earlier this century, a survey was made of mistletoe growing in Britain. One thousand infested trees were examined in various parts of the country. There was not a single oak among

Plate 20. A rare sight. Mistletoe high up on an old wayside oak.
The tree has been damaged by lightning.

them! It was found chiefly on members of the rose family (apple and common hawthorn) and on elm, lime and poplar.

Then why do so many people couple mistletoe and oak together? Probably they have been told that the ancient Druids used mistletoe cut from oak-trees. Perhaps another kind of oak lived in Britain long ago and the mistletoe—or something like it—grew on this. Today, a parasite related to mistletoe is common on a species of oak which lives on the continent but not here.

Nevertheless, we should keep a sharp look-out for mistletoe growing on oak. It does occur (plate 20). If we find it, we can be sure that we are seeing something remarkable.

Mistletoe, and epiphytes, contain chlorophyll. They make either a great deal, or all, of their own food. But the plants which are most closely linked with the oak have no chlorophyll whatever. Being unable to use the sunlight for food-making, they have to feed in other ways.

Plants without chlorophyll

Nearly all of these are fungi of various kinds. (See also page 114.) Many oak fungi—for example the ambrosias (page 88)—are very small. Others, like the poor-man's beefsteak (*Fistulina hepatica*), which we sometimes notice as a sort of shelf jutting out from an oak-trunk, are visible from afar. Their connection with the oak depends on several things.

Some of them feed on old stumps. Others feed on the ground among rotting leaves and waste fragments which have fallen from the oak. These plants are *saprophytes* (*sapros* = rotten, *phyton* = plant) and take dead matter which is decaying. In addition, there are *parasites* which feed on the tree while it is alive. The tree is the parasites' *host*. Some of these fungi 'add insult to injury'. As parasites, they kill their host—then, as saprophytes, they feed on its dead remains.

So many fungi are associated with the oak in one way or

another that only a few of them can be given here. We should also look back to page 96.

One of the most serious destroyers is the honey-fungus (*Armillaria melea*). It attacks conifers as well as trees with broad leaves. When it appears on oaks, its victims seem mostly to be trees weakened already by other diseases. It spreads by dark-coloured hyphae running between the bark and wood. After its host has died, it continues to feed as a saprophyte on the dead material. Its yellowish caps (toadstools) are edible.

Various bracket-fungi occur on oak. Their caps are fan-shaped and often large, and project into the open through the bark. Most of the body of the fungus lies deep inside the tree's tissues. Some kinds are very destructive.

Grifola sulphurea, which has thick, yellow brackets, is a serious cause of decay. Related species usually develop near the base of the trunk. *G. gigantea* has caps which look something like brown leather. They grow in a cluster which may be up to a metre across. Thick masses of much smaller caps which overlap one another and are greyish brown in colour are likely to be those of *G. frondosa* or *G. umbellata*. If they are bruised, the *frondosa* brackets smell of mice.

Poor-man's beefsteak is an edible bracket-fungus. The others mentioned here are not actually poisonous, but are so tough as to be scarcely worth eating. It is shaped something like a hoof or ox-tongue—when cut, its flesh looks and feels like red meat. Its attacks cause 'brown-oak' timber.

Another bracket-fungus, *Daedalea quercina*, is common on the dead boughs of living oaks, or on stumps, and sometimes it grows on gate-posts made of oak. No-one has yet seen it living as a true parasite. Its brackets are corky and quite unfit to eat. On their undersides, they are in folds and ridges.

Not all the parasitic fungi on oak are those producing pale-coloured brackets of toadstools. Two blackish kinds are *Exidia truncata*, which is like a cup, and *Bulgaria inquinans*, looking like flat lumps of indiarubber clustered together.

Saprophytic fungi depending on oak are varied, numerous and widespread. Some, looking like flat sheets of brown honey-comb, are related to the destructive dry-rot fungus (*Serpula lacrymans*), which attacks timber in buildings. Others range from little yellow cups, such as *Helotium* on acorns rotting on the ground, and little yellow drops, like *Dacrymyces deliquescens* which develops on decaying wood after a spell of wet weather, to toad-stools growing on the oak-wood floor.

One of the commonest saprophytes is *Nectria cinnabaria*. We may know its orange-coloured blisters already. They are abundant on the fallen branches of trees of many kinds. Another, *Chloro-splenium aeruginascens*, appears as cups which are actually green, and its hyphae turn decaying oak timber dark green, but the colour is not due to chlorophyll. And *Corticium quercinum* shows up as flat crusts, violet in colour, on the bark of dead boughs.

All these are small, but they grow crowded together and their colouring makes them stand out.

Toadstools are plentiful on woodland floors in autumn. Many we happen to see under oaks actually occur beneath other trees, too. Those which seem to be particularly common in oak-woods include the brownish-red *Russula vesca* and lilac-blue *Contarinius albo-violaceus*. Both are edible. But a related species, *Contarinius anomalus*, which is generally clay-coloured, is valueless as food. Many toadstools are unfit to eat like this. Some are actually poisonous. Two of the most dangerous are the death-cap (*Amanita phalloides*), which is yellowish-green in colour, and the destroying-angel (*A. virosa*), a ghostly-white toadstool.

Unless we have consulted a good reference-book on the subject and are *quite sure* of the actual species, we would be wise to avoid cooking or tasting any toadstools we find.

Just as epiphytes provide part, or all, of the habitats of other

Figure 46. Four fungi which depend on oak: a. poor-man's beefsteak (edible), b. *Russula vesca* (edible), c. destroying angel (highly poisonous), d. *Asterophora parasitica* feeding on *Russula*.

living things, so do fungi. We have already seen how this happens in the case of beetle larvae feeding on the ambrosias. Other beetles, and also numerous fungus-gnats, lay their eggs in the caps of toadstools and bracket-fungi, and their larvae develop here. The most widespread flatbug in Britain, *Aradus depressus*, lives under the bark of oak-trees. It feeds on the hyphae and the caps of various fungi, brackets especially.

Toadstools can even provide food for other toadstools! The little species, *Asterophora parasitica*, feeds and grows on the rotting caps of larger fungi in oak-woods, particularly species of *Russula* and *Lactarius*.

Four of the oak-fungi are drawn in figure 46.

We may be surprised to find a flowering plant without any chlorophyll. Actually, there are several kinds of these. One, the

Figure 47. Bird's-nest orchid: a flowering plant without chlorophyll from the floor of a dark wood.

bird's-nest orchid (*Neottia nidus-avis*), grows in woods. It is fairly common where the soil is chalky and the trees are oak or beech.

The colour of the whole plant, including the flowers, is light fawn. Not being green, it can survive in the deepest shade. Its root-system consists of a dense mass of fibres (the 'bird's nest'). With it, the plant takes in matter coming from foliage which has fallen from the trees and is decaying. It is a saprophyte, but never a parasite. Figure 47 shows some of its features.

131

6. The end of it all

Obviously, the oak is not a tree which lives on its own.

Even if there are no other oaks nearby, the tree has plants depending on it. There are epiphytes, climbers and parasites on its trunk or boughs. There are plants growing in the soil underneath it which survive because of the shade cast by the tree or because of material falling from it. There are animals depending on these plants, or on the oak itself, for food, shelter and somewhere to breed.

Being part of 'the world of a tree', they are members of a *community*.

If the oak-tree is mature, it is likely to shed acorns in autumn. Although the acorns may germinate, the young oaks do not necessarily survive. One reason for this is that man, or his farm animals, may destroy them and leave only the single tree standing. We know that, when the Romans came to Britain 2,000 years ago, they found huge areas of our island covered in dense forests. Man destroyed most of these long ago. Remnants of them still occur here and there, but they are hard to find. Nearly all the woods we see have been planted deliberately.

What sort of community would develop if a piece of land were

132

left alone and plants and animals allowed to invade it naturally? Such an experiment has been carried out in a part of Hertford-shire, where oak-trees grow successfully.

The succession

First the soil was ploughed up and all the remains of plants which could be seen were removed by raking. A fence was erected to keep out grazing or browsing animals which might destroy the vegetation on a large scale. A watch was kept on the bare soil and careful records made of what happened.

Human beings introduced nothing deliberately. At first, a great variety of plants appeared which had soft stems (herbs). There were many species. Most of them germinated, grew, flowered, seeded and died within a few months. These were *annuals* and were the pioneers. As they died off, they were re-placed by others. At first, there were open spaces between the plants. The pioneers, in fact, formed an *open* community. But, as time went by, the gaps became filled in by new arrivals and the situation developed into a *closed* community. A high pro-portion of the pioneers were species whose fruits or seeds were adapted for dispersal by the wind.

Gradually the annuals became replaced by plants which lived longer. These were either *biennials*, surviving for two years, or *perennials*, surviving for more than two. Like the annuals, the biennials were herbs. But they were able to exploit a small area of soil more efficiently. They included plants of the thistle type. In their first year, these produced a large rosette of leaves lying flat against the ground. Such foliage smothered their competitors, including annuals. Having gained the soil for themselves, they sent up in the following season a tall stalk bearing flowers. They reproduced and then died in their second year.

The perennials were varied. Some were herbs, but woody plants appeared as well. Many of these became shrubs. As they developed, they influenced the herbs growing underneath them so that some species died away and new ones took their places. Then young trees were noticed. Many of the shrubs and trees were kinds more likely to have been brought in by birds, or other animals crossing the fence, than by wind. As they grew the trees, too, influenced nearby plants—shrubs and herbs alike— and the species continued to change.

A change of this sort, where some species are followed by others, is *succession*.

Today, a century after the experiment began, the succession has ended in a *woodland community*. Although it was not the first to develop, the principal tree is now pedunculate oak. In the same district are woods which were deliberately created by planting young oak-trees close together and leaving the succession to form naturally. There is very little difference between these woods and the experimental one. The same shrubs and herbs occur in both and the animal life is similar, too. It does not seem to matter in the long run if an oak-wood develops from the

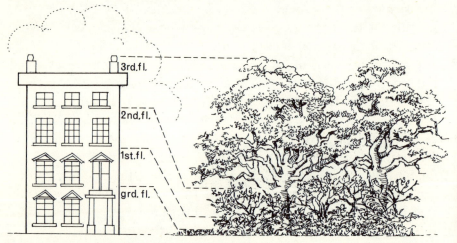

Figure 48. How an oak-wood resembles a house with four storeys.

top downwards (planted wood) or from the bottom upwards (experimental wood).

Changes in succession have largely come to a stop inside a mature oak-wood. As plants and animals die, they are replaced mostly by new individuals of their own species. Such replacements are not succession. A climax has been reached and the community is a stable one. There is a sort of balance between the various organisms—the balance of nature—so that no animal or plant increases to become a pest for long. In any district, the climax is dominated (controlled) by the biggest plants which can grow in the local conditions. In fact, it is a *climatic climax*. Over much of southern Britain, the climax is woodland and oak is the dominant plant.

The climatic climax

The community is not a mixture of organisms merely jumbled up together anyhow. If we visit a well-grown oak-wood, we can see for ourselves that the plants grow in layers. In fact, the wood looks something like a house with four storeys (figure 48).

a. Tree layer. Third floor. Here are the dominant plants— the oaks—exercising the greatest influence over everything in the wood. There may be other trees among them.

b. Shrub layer. Second floor. These are the kinds of bushes which can survive in the conditions produced by the trees above them, by the soil, and by the climate of the district. They are very varied.

Hazel (*Corylus avellana*) is both widespread and common. It reproduces with the aid of wind and is independent of insects.

Midland hawthorn (*Crataegus oxyacanthoides*) is often present. It is pollinated by insects. It flowers a fortnight earlier than common hawthorn (*C. monogyna*) growing in the open, and before the oak foliage conceals its blossoms so that the insects miss them.

135

Plate 21. Female poplar hawk-moth (wing-span, 8·2 cms) from willows in a damp oak-wood.

Honeysuckle, climbing over other shrubs or the trees, comes into flower after the oak-leaves have expanded. Its flowers are strongly scented, especially at night. They are pollinated by moths which fly after sundown and find them by smell.

On clayey soil in the south-east, hornbeam (*Carpinus betulus*) is an oakwood shrub. It casts a shade which is too deep for many species of herbs to grow beneath it.

Elder (*Sambucus nigra*) frequently grows below trees where rooks are nesting. It flourishes where the soil contains plenty of nitrogen. Birds' droppings enrich the soil in this way.

And willow shrubs (*Salix*) may grow in patches of wet ground. The commonest hawk-moth in Britain, the poplar hawk (*Laothoe populi*)—plate 21—sometimes feeds as a caterpillar on willows instead of poplars and occurs in oak-woods of this kind.

c. Herb layer. First floor. Usually a layer of lush plants of many species growing close together. Most of them are perennials. They differ a good deal from place to place inside the wood. All are herbs which can tolerate conditions underneath the particular woody plants near to them.

Bird's-nest orchids can survive even in the shade produced by hornbeam shrubs.

Stinging-nettle (*Urtica dioica*), like elder, does well in nitrogen-rich soil. There are frequently dense masses below rooks' nests or where the trees are used by starlings for roosting.

Many of the herbs—e.g. primrose (*Primula vulgaris*) and blue-bell (*Endymion non-scriptus*)—have bright flowers which open before the woody plants come into leaf and hide them from insects.

d. Moss layer. Ground floor. A mixture of low-growing mosses and leafy liverworts close to the soil just underneath the foliage of the herbs. They seem to need the particularly damp conditions which prevail here.

Thus, the end of it all is a community of numerous organisms dominated by the oak. They are linked together. It is a well-balanced community which will survive just so long as nothing happens to upset the balance. Destruction of oak-trees is more likely than anything else to disturb it. Tidying-up, involving the clearance of dead stumps and other debris, also affects it. This sort of thing has been going on for so long that we are being forced more and more to seek for places of refuge where oakwood organisms remain.

The last refuge

Two examples of these places are hedgerows and the remnants of old forests.

We may not be able to visit a wood, but we may find instead an old and well-grown hedgerow containing oak-trees. A hedge-row of this sort is worth examining. It resembles the margin of a wood. It receives more light—even so, it has many of the features of the oakwood climax. A thick hedgerow shows the four layers. It is often a refuge for woodland organisms which used to be plentiful in the old days, before forests were cleared.

Even where hedgerows are preserved, they are not always as effective as they might be. Great areas of Cambridgeshire, for instance, are as deficient in hedgerows as they are in trees (page 41). Much of the land is used for corn. Hedges have been destroyed and huge fields created which are convenient to manage by farmers who grow corn. Such fields look like the Canadian prairies on a small scale. Hedgerows have been left here and there to give shelter. This is encouraged by the government.

Plate 22. Rocks with soil in crevices but too exposed to sea-spray for trees to survive. *Isle of May*.

They recommend that a farmer who cultivates 100 hectares of crops should preserve at least 1–2 hectares of land as cover. However, there is a risk of these preserved shelters becoming isolated from each other. There need to be connecting hedgerows between them. Otherwise, many animals—snails and woodlice are examples—cannot move from one to another if the conditions change. Birds have less difficulty and can fly many miles across country to reach new sites.

Oak-woods exist in valleys in some of the bleakest and loneliest parts of Dartmoor. They are unlikely to have been planted here by human beings. Evidently they have descended from oaks growing in these places during prehistoric times. Their trees are protected in two ways.

Firstly, they escape the full force of the winds through being established on a sheltered slope of the valley, often on one facing west. Secondly, the trees emerge from the soil between rocks lying on the moor. In its early stages of growth, the young shoot is sheltered by the rock crevices. By the time it has risen above their cover, the little tree is strong enough to withstand the winds. But there are situations which are too exposed for this to happen: an example is given in plate 22.

These woods are weird-looking relics. All the oaks are stunted and never seem to grow much taller than 5–6 metres, no matter how old they become. Their trunks are bent and twisted, or a single oak may have several trunks—probably the result of injury when it was young. High winds can cause distortion and injury. Few shrubs grow beneath these deformed oaks, although some occur beyond the woodland margins. Herbs and mosses are thick but there are not many species. Nevertheless typical oakwood organisms do occur. Epiphytes are luxuriant over the boughs and trunks. Even marble-galls caused by the introduced cynipid *Andricus kollari* (page 71) are plentiful in some of the woods. And a few of our native gall-causers also survive.

139

Plate 23. Ancient oak-wood, Dartmoor, from the south (distance, 2 kilometres). It is growing on a rock-strewn slope sheltered from the west, north and east by high moorland. *Wistman's Wood, Two Bridges.*

Wistman's Wood, probably the most famous of these ancient remnants, appears in plates 23 and 24.

If 'the world of a tree' is not to be lost to us, we need to think carefully about the way we manage our trees. They may be big and impressive, but nowadays they are easily ruined. An oak which has taken centuries to develop can be felled in a matter of hours. Trees are part of our heritage. Many of us probably agree that they look fine, are valuable as material for making things, and are useful in preventing erosion. But there is more to consider than this. On a tree depends a community of living organisms. They, also, are part of our heritage. Like all living things, they are impossible to replace if they become too rare.

And if we merely shrug all this off and declare that there is

Plate 24. Inside the wood. Although the oaks are partly sheltered by rocks, the site is so exposed they remain stunted at 5–6 metres. Note the epiphytes. *Wistman's Wood, Two Bridges.*

only one thing that really matters—getting enough money for our pleasures—we should remember John Ruskin. A hundred years ago this great Englishman saw the truth when he wrote:

'There is no wealth but life'.

7. The study of an individual tree

Reading our book may encourage us to undertake the study of a single oak-tree. If we select our tree wisely and keep careful records, there is much to be learned from such a project. Some of our discoveries may give information which no-one has found out before. There are several ways of planning the investigation. One is suggested here.

Aims

1. To study the structure and life-history of a single tree, and record the changes which take place during a period of one year or longer.
2. To investigate the animals and plants living in association with this tree.
3. To compare 1 and 2 for several oaks of the same species growing in different situations, or for oaks of different species growing in the same situation.

Method

1. If possible, select an isolated tree. Record its position with regard to other trees and buildings, and note its exposure to sun, wind, rain, etc.

Estimate its age and record its height, the diameter of its trunk at various levels, and the spread of its branches.

Record the dates when its leaves start to expand, become fully expanded, its flowers develop, the dispersal of its acorns takes place, and its leaves fall.

Record the growth in length of shoots in different parts of the tree.

Make measurements of the range of leaf-shapes and sizes.

Make rubbings or plaster-casts of the bark.

Collect a sample of the acorns, try to grow them, and calculate the percentage which germinate successfully.

2. Record epiphytic and parasitic plants on the tree. Take into account the position, and the extent and height above the ground, of each species.

By searching and beating, investigate the invertebrates at, say, four set times during the year. Breed eggs, larvae and pupae for identification.

Record mammals and birds associated with the oak at various times of the year. Note their nesting dates, feeding habits, etc.

Record all galls and note whereabouts on the tree each species occurs.

3. Support as many records as possible with drawings and photographs.

Special problems

Probably the greatest difficulty lies in identifying the various animals and plants associated with the tree. The suggestions on pages 145 and 146 may help us. But even if we cannot give an actual name to a particular organism, we need not worry too much. We can give it a number or a letter and draw it for future reference. After all, names should be our servants, not our masters.

Over-collecting by any method must be avoided, and the collecting of birds' eggs never undertaken.

Reasonable care in tree-climbing is obvious, but it can be forgotten in the excitement of a new discovery.

8. Suggestions for further reading

Some splendid guides to natural history have been written for young readers, and the number is going up all the time. We should have little difficulty in finding references to tell us more about the organisms which particularly interest us. There are so many good books that only a small selection can be given here. All are recommended for being easy to understand, having plenty of information, and being well illustrated.

Probably some of the books are in our school library already. If not, we can borrow them from our local lending library. Should we wish to buy our own copies, we are likely to find them —together with other useful publications—on the natural history shelves of most large bookshops.

Young Specialist Series (Burke). Very good aids to identification. There are many titles. One example is

Koch, Alois (1964) *The Young Specialist Looks at Trees and Shrubs.*

Colour Series (Blandford Press). Some are European books which have been translated into English. All are illustrated in excellent colour, and there are short notes on the habits, etc. of the animals. Two dealing with invertebrates, some of which are associated with oak, are

Lyneborg, L. (1968) *Field and Meadow Life*
Mandahl-Barth, G. (1966) *Woodland Life.*

Oxford Pocket Series (O.U.P.) We may find these summaries more and more useful as we grow older. Although small enough to be slipped into the pocket on rambles, they are remarkably detailed. Two titles which include references to oakwood animals are

Sandars, E. (1944) *A Beast Book for the Pocket*, which is about every sort of animal with a backbone except fishes and birds; and

Sandars, E. (1946) *An Insect Book for the Pocket*, which deals with all the orders of insects likely to occur in oak-woods, and also includes such forms as spiders, centipedes, millipedes and woodlice, which are not insects.

Observer's Pocket Series (Warne). Inexpensive and excellent value. So many different subjects are included that most features of oakwood life are likely to be covered. Four of the titles are

Benson, S. Vere (1966) *Birds*
Jewell, A. (1964) *Mosses and Liverworts*
Kershaw, K. A. and Alvin, K. L. (1963) *Lichens*
Wakefield, E. M. (1961) *Fungi.*

Wayside and Woodland Series (Warne). As in the Observer's Series, by the same publisher, there are many titles. The books are larger and more detailed. Like the Oxford Series, we shall probably find them increasingly useful as we grow up.

Life Nature Library. All are full of information and contain photographs which are outstandingly good.

Survival Books. A new series based on the television programmes 'Survival'. Each book deals with a different species, or group of species.

Index

English and scientific names of the living things mentioned in this book.

Index